# the food and cooking of
# Malaysia & Singapore

# the food and cooking of
# Malaysia & Singapore

Discover an exotic cuisine that blends
Malay, Indian and Chinese traditions,
with 80 recipes and over 300 photographs

## Ghillie Başan

with photography by Martin Brigdale

aqua marine

# To Peter, the adopted Dyak. Selamat makan!

This edition is published by Aquamarine

Aquamarine is an imprint of Anness Publishing Ltd
Hermes House, 88–89 Blackfriars Road, London SE1 8HA
tel. 020 7401 2077; fax 020 7633 9499

www.aquamarinebooks.com; info@anness.com

© Anness Publishing Ltd 2006

UK agent: The Manning Partnership Ltd, 6 The Old Dairy,
Melcombe Road, Bath BA2 3LR; tel. 01225 478444; fax 01225 478440;
sales@manning-partnership.co.uk

UK distributor: Grantham Book Services Ltd, Isaac Newton Way,
Alma Park Industrial Estate, Grantham, Lincs NG31 9SD; tel. 01476 541080;
fax 01476 541061; orders@gbs.tbs-ltd.co.uk

North American agent/distributor: National Book Network,
4501 Forbes Boulevard, Suite 200, Lanham, MD 20706;
tel. 301 459 3366; fax 301 429 5746; www.nbnbooks.com

Australian agent/distributor: Pan Macmillan Australia, Level 18,
St Martins Tower, 31 Market St, Sydney, NSW 2000; tel. 1300 135 113;
fax 1300 135 103; customer.service@macmillan.com.au

New Zealand agent/distributor: David Bateman Ltd, 30 Tarndale Grove,
Off Bush Road, Albany, Auckland; tel. (09) 415 7664; fax (09) 415 8892

A CIP catalogue record for this book is available from the British Library.

Publisher: Joanna Lorenz
Editorial Director: Judith Simons
Senior Editor: Doreen Gillon
Editor: Molly Perham
Stylist: Helen Trent
Home Economists: Lucy McKelvie and Bridget Sargeson
Designer: Simon Daley
Cover Designer: Chloe Steers
Editorial Reader: Penelope Goodare
Production Manager: Steve Lang

10 9 8 7 6 5 4 3 2 1

Main front cover image shows Sarawak *sambal udang*, for recipe
see page 88

## Notes

Bracketed terms are intended for American readers.

For all recipes, quantities are given in both metric and imperial measures
and, where appropriate, in standard cups and spoons. Follow one set, but
not a mixture; they are not interchangeable.

Standard spoon and cup measures are level.
1 tsp = 5ml, 1 tbsp = 15ml, 1 cup = 250ml/8fl oz.

Australian standard tablespoons are 20ml. Australian readers should
use 3 tsp in place of 1 tbsp for measuring small quantities of
gelatine, flour, salt, etc.

American pints are 16fl oz/2 cups. American readers should use 20fl oz/2.5
cups in place of 1 pint when measuring liquids.

The nutritional analysis given for each recipe is calculated per portion (i.e.
serving or item), unless otherwise stated. If the recipe gives a range, such as
Serves 4–6, then the nutritional analysis will be for the smaller portion size,
i.e. 6 servings. Measurements for sodium do not include salt added to taste.

Medium (US large) eggs are used unless otherwise stated.

## Acknowledgements

First a big thank you to the two little joys in my life, Yasmin and Zeki.
Among all the friendly faces in Malaysia and Singapore, there are always so
many people to thank but I couldn't get away without mentioning Peter
Grant of Frank's, Singapore, for all his help in circumnavigating the food
stalls; Daisy Solomon from the Beach Restaurant on the island of Labuan;
Mamat Dagan in Terengganu and his mother who makes the most
wonderful anchovy dishes; Usop Omar, the "durian king", from Miri in
Sarawak; Ravinder Singh in Kuala Lumpur; Joseph Toyo in Kota Kinabolu; and
the Dyak chief, Ambu Gang, also known as the "kayubala" (timber king) and
last of the headhunters in Sarawak.

For background research I was thankful to have the *Lonely Planet Malaysia,
Singapore & Brunei* to keep me informed, the outstanding volume *Essentials
of Asian Cuisine* by Corinne Trang, and the classic *South East Asian Food* by
Rosemary Brissenden. My thanks also go to Doreen Gillon and the team at
Aquamarine, and to William Lingwood for his superb photography.
Seasoned Pioneers, as usual, came up trumps with their excellent spices.

## Publisher's acknowledgements

The publisher would like to thank William Lingwood for his stunning
photography throughout the book, apart from the following images:
Arcangel Images pages 8bl, 10tr; Nicki Dowey pages 10bl, 11, 20, 22bl, 22bc,
42, 113br; Robert Harding Picture Library pages 7br, 8br, 15t, 16, 18, 26, 77t;
Superstock Ltd pages 15br, 17, 19, 23, 60; Travel-ink pages 7t, 9, 12, 13, 14, 93br.

# Contents

# Introduction

The rich variety of culinary traditions found throughout South-east Asia come together in Malaysia and Singapore. From Chinese businessmen in skyscrapers in Kuala Lumpur to Orang Asli hunter-gatherers in the hilly jungles of the Malay peninsula, the people and their eating habits are as diverse as the landscape. Thanks to its geographical position, on the sea routes of the ancient civilizations of Asia, India and China, the area has been influenced by invaders, merchants and immigrants from far and wide.

It was only in the 1960s that Malaysia and Singapore emerged as independent countries. Malaysia was born in 1963, with the merging of Malaya, Singapore, Sabah and Sarawak, while Brunei remained separate. However, Singapore's marriage with Malaysia was not a happy one. It broke free in 1965 and has succeeded as a small nation since, with an emphasis on hard work and a tight economy.

The cultural mix of Malaysia and Singapore is so diverse that it reads like a recipe in itself. The population of Malaysia is about 60 per cent Malay, 26 per cent Chinese and 7 per cent Indian, with a dash of Peranakan, Eurasian, Indonesian and tribal influences, and garnished with Vietnamese, Japanese, Filipino and Thai. Most Malays are followers of Islam, as well as adhering to old spiritual beliefs and systems of social law. In the *kampung* (Malay village), the early Hindu-based system of *adat*, with an emphasis on collective responsibility, is part of everyday life. Obligations of kinship and social harmony are at the heart of the Malay psyche, so much so that many urban Malays, caught up in the busy whirl of Kuala Lumpur and Singapore, miss the spiritual simplicity of *kampung* life.

In Singapore, the pace of life is fast and urban. The population is 76 per cent Chinese, 15 per cent Malay and 6 per cent Indian, with a small number of Peranakan, Eurasian and Indonesian, sprinkled with Western influences. What this all adds up to is one of the most colourful and exciting culinary scenes in the world, made all the more tangible with the fascinating tradition of hawker stalls, where exotic food from each of these cultures can be sampled in one place.

## Malayan ancestry

The Orang Asli, the aboriginal Malays, provide us with the most vivid evidence of the early Malay culinary culture. Believed to have migrated 10,000 years ago from the region in China where the great rivers of South-east Asia meet (today's Qinghai Province), the Orang Asli settled in the peninsula forests where they led a hunter-gatherer existence. The numbers have dwindled considerably, and some have intermarried with other ethnic groups, but there are still pockets of hunter-gatherer Orang Asli in the hilly jungles of Pahang.

Other Malay descendants who settled on the peninsula were said to be of the same ethnic group as their

**Left** *Modern-day Malaysia is divided into the two distinct regions of West and East, covering 329,758sq km/ 127,320sq miles. West Malaysia (the Malay peninsula) is joined to mainland Asia with Singapore at the bottom. East Malaysia encompasses the northern part of Borneo and is divided into two states, Sabah and Sarawak.*

**Above** *Fishermen setting their nets at sunrise in the calm waters off Langkawi, the legendary island off the north-west coast of Malaysia.*

...........................................

Indonesian ancestors. Culturally they were similar, particularly when it came to food and culinary traditions: this common bond still exists, as the Malays and Indonesians share many of the same spicy dishes. As the Malay ancestors settled on the peninsula, some moved inland and married Orang Asli women, spreading their knowledge of rice cultivation and the beasts of burden, the ox and water buffalo.

Over in East Malaysia, Sabah and Sarawak are still home to numerous tribal groups, who fish, hunt and collect wild plants and herbs, most of which are peculiar to those regions.

## The story of Melaka

A turning point in the region's culinary importance was around 1400, when the fishing village of Melaka grew into a significant port. With Indian ships sailing in on the south-west monsoon and Chinese junks being blown in by the north-west monsoon, Melaka boomed as a multicultural trade centre, drawing traders, merchants and missionaries to its shores.

The local cooking was influenced by the arrival of new cooking techniques and spices, such as cardamom, pepper, cloves and exotic fruits and vegetables. When the sultan of Melaka converted to Islam in the mid-15th century, there

...........................................

**Right** *Traditional houses of the Orang Asli people in the hilly jungles of Pahang, central Malaysia.*

was an increase in traders from Indonesia and the Middle East, which had a lasting effect on the Malay food culture.

Melaka's colourful history has left an enviable culinary heritage. Malay,

Chinese, Peranakan and Eurasian cuisines all flourish in Melaka, with a particular emphasis on spices and creamy coconut milk. The sago pudding soaked in palm sugar syrup, *sagu gula melaka*, is a Malay favourite, as is *satay celup*, an assortment of skewered food, such as shellfish, vegetables, fish balls, hard-boiled quail's eggs and chunks of chicken or beef, which is cooked in boiling stock, like a Swiss fondue, and served with a peanut sauce. Satay is likely to have evolved from the Middle Eastern kebab, brought to the region by Muslim Indian or Arab traders.

**Below** *A trader preparing fresh fish for sale at his stall in a typical Malaysian open-air market.*

## Typical Malay meals

At the heart and soul of Malay food is the *rempah*, a spice paste made by first pounding wet ingredients such as shallots, ginger, garlic and chilli, and then adding dry spices such as coriander seeds, cardamom and ground turmeric, to form a mixture that is cooked in oil before any of the other ingredients are added. Rice is usually at the root of a Malay meal, either cooked plain or flavoured with coconut milk or spices. Traditional rice dishes include *ketupat*, pressed rice cooked in coconut fronds, and *lemang*, rice stuffed into hollow bamboo tubes lined with banana leaves and cooked over a charcoal fire.

Generally, a Malay meal consists of a fish or shellfish curry, or a meat or chicken dish, served with rice, a vegetable dish and a chilli sambal. Bread is often served instead of rice, particularly in dishes with lots of richly flavoured sauce that begs to be mopped up with fresh, crusty baguette. The Malays also enjoy the Indian flat, flaky bread, *roti paratha*, with curries, or as a snack, sprinkled with sugar.

## Penang: gastronomic heaven

Off the mainland, the small island of Penang grew as a major trade centre under the East India Company in the 18th and 19th centuries, when it was one of the best sources of nutmeg and

**Below** *Passenger and produce boats moored along the banks of the busy Malay river.*

**Right** *A Chinese market at Penang, the Pearl of the Orient.*

cloves. At this time it attracted immigrants from China, Sumatra, Thailand, Burma and India. The intermingling of these varied cultures is reflected in the food of Penang, which is regarded as a gastronomic heaven.

Specialities include the Indian-inspired *murtabak*, flatbread filled with spicy minced (ground) beef or lamb and vegetables; Peranakan *pasembur*, a salad of shredded yam, bean, tofu, cuttlefish and cucumber tossed with beansprouts and prawn (shrimp) fritters in a sweet and sour dressing; *Penang asam laksa*, the local noodles in coconut milk, with flakes of mackerel, garnished with pineapple, cucumber, chilli, mint and shrimp paste; and *pong piah*, a Hokkien dish of flaky puff pastry filled with a milky syrup.

The Indian coffee shops in Penang are also famous for their pulled tea, *teh tarik*, which is deliciously sweet and frothy. It is usually made by an Indian man who pours the sweetened tea from a metal pot held above his head into another one held below his waist and repeats the process several times until a layer of froth has formed on the surface and the tea has cooled to drinking temperature, when it is poured into the cup. Also known descriptively as *teh terbang*, which translates as "flying tea", this is an acquired art and the tea is just as popular with locals as it is with tourists.

## Indian contributions

The Indians had traded in the region long before the Europeans set up colonies. However, it was not until the 19th century, when the British brought them in to provide cheap labour in the rubber plantations, that the Indian culture had a strong influence on the cuisine of the region. Most of these Indians are Hindus from South India, where rice and dhal (lentils) are the staples and food is eaten with the hands. Hindus don't eat beef and many are vegetarian, so they introduced vegetable dishes and pickles to the Malays. Southern Indians also tend to cook with coconut oil, contrasting with the ghee-based dishes of North India, such as *tandoori* and *biryani*.

The most distinctive style of Indian cooking is that found at the *mamak* (Indian Muslim) hawker stalls, particularly in Singapore, where the cooks combine Malay and Indian flavours and techniques. The resulting spicy dishes are in a class of their own, such as *mee rebus*, thick fresh egg noodles in a sweet, spicy sauce served with eggs and chillies, and *rojak*, a crispy vegetable salad with fried tofu and fish cakes in a spicy-sweet sauce. A feature of Indian food that stands out from the rest is the use of yogurt as a cooling accompaniment to hot curries, either served plain, or mixed with vegetables and herbs in a *raita* or *pachadi*, or blended in *lassi*, a refreshing yogurt drink.

**Below** *Satay is a popular dish at food stalls in Malaysia and Singapore. Grilled over charcoal, it is traditionally served with peanut sauce.*

## Chinese dishes

Like the Indians, Chinese traders had had a long history with the region, but it wasn't until the 19th century that the population grew. With the increase in the region's tin mining and agriculture, the numbers of Chinese grew so quickly that, by 1827, they formed the largest single community in Singapore. By 1845, they made up half the population. Tremendous farmers, the Chinese were responsible for planting many of the rice paddies and vegetable plantations in the region. Hailing from the provinces of Guangdong, Fujian and Guangxi, they belonged to different socio-linguistic groups, such as Teochew, Hokkien and Hainanese, each of which adheres to its own traditions and cuisines.

Traditionally, rice has always been the staple of Chinese cooking. The Chinese do not waste any part of any living creature, and rice can be served with anything from duck's feet to dog to sea cucumber. In Malaysia and

**Above** *Customers waiting to be served at a street stall in Singapore selling Hainanese specialities.*

Singapore, the Chinese communities still eat much the same as their ancestors, based on the same principles of yin and yang, sweet and sour, hot and cold, and plain and spicy.

The Indian and Malay influence has in turn made an impact on some of their traditional dishes, particularly those served at hawker stalls in Singapore. Spicy favourites include *char kway teow*, stir-fried rice noodles with prawns (shrimp), squid and Chinese sausage, and Hainanese chicken rice, which is served with a dish of chillies on the side to satisfy the Malay palate. A legacy of the 19th-century colonial period, when the British acquired Malaya and Singapore, is the addition of Western ingredients. The British "cookboys" were generally Hainanese, so tomato ketchup and Worcestershire sauce appear among the ingredients of some Chinese dishes.

## The Nonya cuisine

When the early Chinese traders began to settle in the ports of Penang, Melaka and Singapore from the 15th century onward, a number of them married local Malay women to create an ethnic sub-group of Malay-Chinese. In Malay, this group is called Peranakan, which means "half caste", but they also refer to themselves as Straits Chinese to distinguish themselves from the Chinese immigrants who came later.

Using the Peranakan words for male (*baba*) and female (*nonya*), this group was also referred to as the Baba-Nonyas, and was noted for its distinct colourful dress and lavishly decorated homes and, above all, its cuisine. As the Peranakans were relatively wealthy, they were able to indulge in elaborate meals prepared by the women, developing the unique Nonya cuisine, an inspired mix of Chinese and Malay traditions.

To this day, Nonya cooking is highly praised and much sought after with its lavish use of chillies, lemon grass, galangal and turmeric fused with a splash of Indian, Thai, Portuguese and Chinese cooking methods. Classic Nonya dishes include *mee siam*, a Thai-influenced dish of rice noodles in a spicy, tangy sauce, and *babi pong tey*, a pork stew cooked in an earthenware pot. It is worth looking out for Nonya *tok panjang*, which translates as "Nonya long table". It consists of an elaborate buffet spread of Nonya specialities. The style of eating is similar to Malay, as most dishes are served with rice, or bread, and accompanied by a chilli sambal or a bowl of fiery chillies.

## Eurasian hybrid cooking

In the 16th century, Portuguese traders and explorers colonized parts of Malaysia, particularly Melaka, and

married local women. The descendants called themselves Jenti Cristang (Christian people) and spoke their own language, a kind of Creole Portuguese. They were also called Eurasian, along with the descendants of other mixed European-Malay unions, and developed their own cuisine, a hybrid of Malay, Chinese, Peranakan and Indian, combined with Portuguese cooking methods.

The European influence can be noted in their love of roasted cuts of meat, grilled chops and steaks.

**Above** *A market seller sorting chillies.*

However, exotic curries, with sour notes of tamarind and lime, are also Eurasian top favourites, including the fiery devil's curry, *curry debal*, and the Christmas pork curry, *feng*. Curries and other savoury dishes are usually served with rice or bread but, unlike the other culinary cultures of Malaysia and Singapore, the Eurasians enjoy a dessert at the end of a meal.

# Regional variations

The people of Malaysia and Singapore are proud of their diverse culinary cultures and regional food. In Singapore, you can eat just about anything, from traditional Hainanese chicken rice to contemporary chilli crab, as it is a melting pot of all culinary cultures and a gourmet delight. Each group eats the same dish in a slightly different way, adjusting the balance to suit their taste, such as the Malay desire for a chilli kick with every mouthful. In rural Malaysia the food is much more regionalized.

In Kedah and Perlis, the rice-growing regions in the north of the Malay peninsula, the Thai influence is evident; Ipoh is well known for its authentic Chinese food, due to the immigrant population that worked in the tin mines; Penang and Melaka are famed for their delicious Nonya dishes; and Kelantan is regarded as pure Malay. In Sabah and Sarawak, fish dishes are common fare and sago palm provides the main carbohydrate. Tribal hunters track wild boar and deer for the table and jungle ferns and their shoots are collected for vegetable stir-fries.

## The Malaysian peninsula

Bordering Thailand in the north of the peninsula, the two states, Perlis and Kedah, are known as the region's rice bowl, producing over half of the country's domestic rice supply. Given its proximity to Thailand and the influx of Thais settling in the region, the local cuisine is inevitably influenced by hot, spicy flavours paired with sourness – the Thai culinary trademark. The local fishermen and rice farmers favour simple fish dishes, flavoured with chillies, lemon grass, kaffir lime leaves, lime juice and fish sauce. They are often tempered with a sweet prawn (shrimp) sauce, *otak udang*, and served with refreshing herbs and shredded cucumber.

Further down the west coast to the states of Perak and Selangor, and the capital city, Kuala Lumpur, the food is much more varied, influenced in succession by Indian traders, Chinese merchants, European colonizers, immigrant workers and 20th-century industrialization.

Kuala Lumpur, which has grown from a tin-mining town to an affluent, cosmopolitan capital, is as fascinating as Singapore for its *mélange* of food cultures. You can find regional specialities of Malaysia, India and China; you can enter the international restaurant scene and sample the French, Vietnamese and Japanese high-class fare; you can seek out old colonial haunts serving British breakfasts and fried chicken with Worcestershire sauce; or you can follow the young crowd and wait at the hawker stalls for instant noodles with fried egg on top.

**Left** *The fertile Cameron Highlands attracted an influx of planters and farmers and, as a result, vegetables, flowers and tea bushes grow in profusion in the plateaux and foothills.*

Much of Malaysia's tea is grown in the plantations in Perak's highlands, which lead into the Cameron Highlands inside Pahang. Named after the surveyor who mapped the area in 1885, the Cameron Highlands consist of a network of jungles and waterfalls with fertile plateaux, which attracted tea planters, Chinese and Malay vegetable farmers and wealthy colonialists who retreated from the heat of the lowlands to highland hill stations. Much of Pahang has remained impenetrable to prospectors and planters, dividing the east and west of the Malaysian peninsula with its high mountain ridges, but it is the domain of the Orang Asli who thrive in the jungles and rely on simple, easily acquired food. Tapioca and rice form the staples and fish provides the protein. Malaysia's longest river, Sungai Pahang, flows right through the state and its tributaries are full of plump carp and catfish.

Over on the east coast, the states of Kelantan and Terengganu are steeped in Malay culture. Separated from the industrialized west coast by the peaks of Pahang, the coastline is dotted with thriving fishing villages and idyllic pearly beaches. Life moves at a slower pace with fishing as its mainstay. Fish is bought from the nets as the boats come to shore and the local Malay women are inventive with their dishes.

In Terengganu, the savoury pastries, *epok-epok*, are filled with fish and grated coconut, and the local delicacy, *satar,* is made by stuffing banana-leaf cones with a spicy-sour fish paste and grilling them over charcoal. Kelantan boasts some unique specialities, such as *nasi dagang*, red or brown glutinous rice cooked in coconut milk and served with fish, grated coconut, herbs and sauces, and the famous *nasi kerabu*, a rice dish tinted blue with dye from the pea flower, *bunga telang*, which is served with fish crackers and fried salted fish.

In the south of the peninsula, Negeri Sembilan produces seriously fiery dishes, influenced by the Minangkabau who came from Sumatra in the 15th century. The Malay speciality, *rendang*, beef cooked in coconut milk, is held to be best in Negeri Sembilan, where it is served with *lemang*, glutinous rice cooked with coconut milk inside bamboo poles positioned over a fire.

The most southern state on the peninsula is Johor, which, in spite of the influx of Chinese immigrants, has retained a strong Malay culture and cuisine. A local speciality is *Satay Johor,* in which skewered meat is continuously basted with a mixture of coconut milk and oil, brushed on with a lemon grass stalk, which imparts a delicate lemony flavour to the meat. *Laksa Johor* is also popular as the soupy noodles in coconut milk are served with chunks of herring and flavoured with tamarind and fresh mint.

Johor is also known as the pineapple state and provides Singapore with much of its farm produce and water. Linked to Singapore by two causeways, the capital Johor Bahru offers many of the same hawker dishes, such as *char kway teow*, noodles stir-fried with squid, prawn (shrimp) and Chinese sausage in a sweet sauce, and *nasi biryani*, an Indian rice casserole. Many Singaporeans drive over to Johor Bahru for its cheaper versions of their own delicious seafood dishes.

## Singapore

Often referred to as the "Manhattan of the East", Singapore is a consumer's paradise and food is a national obsession. Everywhere you go there is something to eat and everywhere you look people are eating. Food is a constant topic of conversation. Similar to Penang, Kuala Lumpur and Melaka, Singapore is rich in diverse cultures and food traditions, but to many Singaporeans the origin of the dish is unimportant as long as it is tasty. Chinese food rules the roost, followed closely by Malay and Indian.

Most fascinating of all is how the culinary culture of Singapore has evolved. With no agriculture but a great deal of affluence, so that all manner of goods can be imported, the cuisine of the tiny nation has developed from the humble barrow on the street corner, selling one simple dish cooked on a single burner, to some of the most sophisticated hawker stalls in the world. For those who wish to dine in style, the Singapore restaurant scene ranks with the best in Sydney, Paris and New York, as the chefs are always creating something new.

The hawker tradition and coffee shop (*kopi tiam* – similar to a Western café) culture are most popular in Singapore, as many people are busy and live in tiny apartments, so eating out is the obvious choice. For some, cooking at home is only a weekend activity. As Singapore is divided into racial quarters, the hawker stalls and coffee shops follow a similar pattern. In Katong, the Peranakan and Eurasian section, they offer competitive versions of Singapore *laksa*, noodles in coconut milk, right next to coffee shops selling European tea cakes or Chinese chicken rice cafés. In Little India, the warm, spicy aromas of the Tekka Market attract Hindu, Muslim and Chinese shoppers, as well as the Nonyas (Peranakan ladies) and European *taitais* (ladies of leisure) who descend on the Indian coffee shops to tuck into a freshly made *roti paratha* (flaky flatbread), washed down with the sweet pulled tea, *teh tarik*.

Unique to Singapore are the *dosai* shops, which sell Indian rice crêpes, *dosai*, and vegetarian dishes, as they are run by Hindus who do not eat meat. In the same areas you will find Indian "banana leaf" restaurants, where the food is served on banana leaves.

While there are only slight differences between dishes such as Penang and Singapore *laksa*, or Johor and Singapore *char kway teow*, some dishes are unique to Singapore – they may be versions of traditional dishes that have been given a Singapore twist, or new creations by adventurous chefs. One that has become a Singapore classic is stir-fried chilli crab in a tomato sauce, eaten with the fingers and mopped up with French baguette.

## Sabah

The main reasons to visit Malaysia's northernmost state on the island of Borneo are to climb Mount Kinabalu, or to visit the orang-utan rehabilitation centre. However, Sabah is also home to gorgeous deserted beaches, coral reef and wild Asian elephants and rhinos, as well as 30 different ethnic groups who thrive on a diet of fish and shellfish, deer, wild boar and wild plants, herbs and fruit from the forests. Rice is cultivated in the hills, but the main staples of Sabah are corn and tapioca. Sabah's national fish dish, *hinava*, consists of finely sliced raw fish marinated in lime juice and herbs.

The Kadazans, the main tribal community in the west, favour the sour tastes of unripe mangoes, limes and tangy star fruit and are particularly proud of their fish dish, *hinava tongii*, which combines fresh mackerel with chillies, ginger, shallots and lime juice and one special ingredient that makes all the difference – the grated stone (pit) of a local mango, the *bambangan*. Dried shrimps and anchovies are added to many dishes.

**Left** *When visiting high-rise Singapore City, you may taste little difference between a Hainanese curry and a Malay one, but the locals are acutely aware of the different ingredients and techniques.*

In the swamp lands, the wild sago palm provides the indigenous communities with sago pearls for the carbohydrate content of their diet. The Bisaya, a Muslim group, use the sago to make a thick porridge, *ambuyat*, which they dip into a fiery *sambal*. In the hilly south-west, the Murut hunt wild boar, chop up the meat and stuff it, with chunks of freshwater fish, jungle leaves, rice grains and salt, into the hollow of bamboo stems, where the mixture is left to ferment for weeks, even months. This pungent speciality, *jaruk*, is eaten with steamed rice or tapioca. Rice wine, *tapai*, made from glutinous rice and yeast, is enjoyed by the non-Muslim Sabahan tribes.

## Sarawak

Like Sabah, Sarawak is a world apart from the Malaysian peninsula. Covered with dense rainforests, rivers, caves and national parks where wildlife can be spotted, this state is home to the Dayaks, Ibans, Melanau and other indigenous tribes. Longhouses and river excursions through the jungles using head-hunter trails are part of the tourist experience, as is the city of Kuching. Although rice is grown in Sarawak, vast areas of the land are too swampy for paddies, so some tribes rely on the wild sago palm for carbohydrate. A Melanau fisherman's dish, *umai*, consists of finely sliced raw fish, marinated in tamarind or lime juice with chopped shallots, chillies and salt, and served with a bowl of toasted sago pearls. Sago grubs (young caterpillars found in sago palms), stir-fried with shallots, ginger and chillies, are popular among the tribal peoples, and as in Sabah the sago pearls are boiled to make a thick porridge-like paste, which is usually eaten with a fiery *sambal*.

**Right** *Sifting sago pearls into a large vat for making a porridge-like paste.*

**Above** *A Bajau family in their stilt house in Sabah, with fish drying on the platform outside.*

Wild boar and deer are Sarawakan favourites, roasted whole over charcoal, or used for satay dishes, accompanied by vegetable dishes. Most tribes make their own *arak*, a local liquor, and *tuak*, rice wine, which are very potent.

# Stalls, coffee shops & markets

The Malay and Singaporean passionate love of food is evident on the streets wherever you go. In parts of Malaysia, the hawker stall still functions as it always has done – as a portable stove on which one or several dishes were prepared for labourers at the plantations, fishermen and traders at the ports, or for business people and travellers on busy street corners. In the cities, most street carts have now been moved into purpose-built indoor food centres.

Most city-dwellers rely on stall food, lacking the time to cook at home. In Kuala Lumpur and Singapore, high-class, air-conditioned food courts with tables and chairs are often located in shopping malls and at the foot of office buildings. Food halls offer the truly multicultural culinary mix, as adjacent hawker stalls enable diners to taste a bit of Indian, Chinese and Malay at the same meal. But some locals argue that the most authentic food is still to be found at the little stalls on wheels clustered outside markets and coffee shops or by the roadside in rural areas.

### Food to go

Muslim and Malay stalls are often grouped together, selling the Indian-inspired mutton soup, *sop kambing*, the Thai-influenced spicy tangy noodles, *mee siam*, and the traditional Malay rice porridge, *bubur*, served with side dishes such as fried dried anchovies and a chilli *sambal*. At grill stalls you find spicy chicken wings, stingray wings served in banana leaves, and fish, beef, chicken or lamb satay. Rice stalls may offer a selection of dishes with the rice or just one. Some offer specialities such as Hainanese chicken rice.

*Cze cha* stalls generally display a mix of Chinese and Malay snacks, such as noodles in broth, fish balls, stuffed chillies, and dumplings filled with prawns (shrimp) and pork. Noodle stalls lure you with the sweet, spicy aromas of stir-fried prawns and clams, ginger and garlic, as popular dishes such as *char kway teow* are cooked in abundance. Rice cake stalls serve these South Indian specialities with chutneys and *sambals*, which are often devoured for breakfast or a mid-morning snack. Roti stalls also serve Indian specialities, such as the flaky flatbread, *roti paratha*; *murtabak*, which is a flatbread filled with spicy minced (ground) lamb or chicken; and various dhals.

Sweet stalls offer Malay, Chinese, Indian and Peranakan snacks and desserts, such as *gulab jamun*, the Indian deep-fried sweetmeats made with coconut milk, *kueh-kueh*, which are Peranakan tea cakes, and Chinese sweet bean soups. Ice cream is also sold from stalls and small refrigerators attached to bicycles.

Seasonal fruits are displayed at fruit and juice stalls and can be bought in wedges or blended into a drink. Snack

**Left** *A cook preparing a variety of dishes at a busy street stall in Singapore.*

**Right** *A typical Malaysian open-air fruit and vegetable market, resplendent with colour.*

stalls sell roasted chestnuts, salted or sugared *kacang*, which is a mixture of roasted peanuts, peas and beans, deep-fried prawn crackers, deep-fried bananas and *vadai*, *dhal* fritters.

## Coffee and tea

The coffee shop culture in Malaysia and Singapore is friendly and atmospheric. Often housed in the ground floor of old stores and houses, the setup is basic with minimal decoration and plain tables and chairs. Each neighbourhood has its own Chinese, Malay or Indian coffee shop where people gather for a chat and a cup of tea or coffee and, frequently, a meal. Meals served in coffee shops are simple and cultural-specific, such as the fish head soup served in the Indian and Malay premises, or noodles and dim sum in the Chinese.

Some tea shops specialize in the famous pork bone tea, *bak kut teh*. In Singapore, these shops have individual charcoal stoves set up at each table. Kettles are set upon the stoves and left to boil while the *bak kut teh* is served. Teapots and cups are warmed with the boiling water, before Chinese tea leaves are dropped into the teapots and left to brew. This tea is sipped alongside the peppery soup. Strips of tender meat are torn from the bone and dipped into soy sauce infused with chillies.

For breakfast in the coffee shops, popular choices include *roti kaya*, grilled flatbread smeared with coconut egg jam, and *kuay neng*, runny, soft-boiled eggs that are cracked open in a saucer and mixed with soy sauce and ground black pepper.

The principal tea grown in the Malaysian plantations is an Indian Assam variety. Generally, tea is made strong and served sweetened with condensed milk. *Teh tarik*, pulled tea, is a speciality of the region. On hot, muggy days, iced tea is a cooling alternative, and the warm, milky ginger tea, *teh halia*, is regarded as a late-night pick-me-up. Chinese jasmine or lotus teas are served clear in little teacups to enhance the appetite, cleanse the blood or aid digestion.

Coffee begins and ends the day for many Malays. Brewed strong with earthy and mellow characteristics, it is always sweetened with condensed milk. Traditionally, coffee houses roasted and ground their own choice of beans but, nowadays, the preferred varieties, such as the dark-roasted, oily beans from Java and Sumatra, are bought in the markets. In some of the older Singapore coffee houses the custom of adding roasted corn and butter to the sweet brew continues. Sweet, iced coffee is also popular in the Singapore sunshine, and busy workers rely on the crude version of "carry-out" coffee, served in the cleaned-out condensed milk cans.

## Marketplaces

The markets represent the fabulous reality of integrated multiculturalism and culinary fusion, as well as the breathtaking volume and variety of the local produce, all vociferously haggled over. Singapore markets also display imported fruits and vegetables from Australia, Japan, India and Ecuador.

A typical market has wet and dry regions, divided into rows to separate meat from fish, vegetables from fruit, and dried beans and grains from condiments. At the edges, there are stalls selling pots and pans, brooms and mops, clothes and shoes, and makeshift food stalls selling snacks, fruit and drinks. The large central markets stay open all day, the local neighbourhood ones close at midday, and the open-air night markets close around midnight.

# Celebrations

With such a variety of culinary cultures, every religious or family celebration is a banquet of delights. Traditional weddings involve a great deal of feasting, some of which is symbolic and can span several days. Throughout Malaysia and Singapore, births also require ceremonial feasting, which often takes place on the 100th day in Chinese and Peranakan households. Special foods are called for at Chinese New Year, the Muslim Hari Raya Puasa, Indian Diwali, Christmas and other festivals.

## Weddings

At Malay weddings, the feasting is on a huge scale with hundreds of guests who must be served a selection of rice dishes and curries. As they depart, each guest is presented with delicately wrapped gifts of hard-boiled eggs to ensure fertility for the newly-weds. Similarly, Indian weddings operate on a large scale with a vast selection of dishes tailored to the religious and regional groups, such as Bengalis, Punjabis and Tamils, attending.

Chinese weddings are more restrained with a traditional tea ceremony and a family banquet. On an auspicious day, the groom visits the bride's house to pay his respects and ask for her hand. When accepted, the groom and his bride return to his home, where they kneel before his parents and older relatives and serve them a specially brewed tea to symbolize that the bride will undertake her new role of serving and caring for her in-laws. The final banquet is usually supplied by the groom's parents who take traditional gifts of food, such as a suckling pig, to be eaten at the bride's house. In a Peranakan marriage, the bride's future mother-in-law often cooks a special coconut rice dish, *nasi lemak*, which she traditionally takes as an offering to the bride's mother to give reassurance that the bride is still a virgin.

## Christmas

The snow that traditionally accompanies Christmas in northern Europe may not appear in Malaysia and Singapore, but there is no shortage of fake snow, twinkling lights, furs, shiny baubles and silver tinsel. Christmas may be a Eurasian festival, but everyone joins in, from the decorations to the presents and feasting. In Eurasian households, it is common to find roast turkey on the Christmas table – stuffed with glutinous rice, pork and chestnuts. Honey-baked hams keep up the Western traditions, but are often accompanied by chicken or pork curries, such as *curry debal* and *feng*, which is made a day in advance to enhance the flavour. With such a colourful European and Malay heritage, the Eurasians draw from all their different influences at Christmas, adding soy-based dishes, chilli dips, steamed cabbage rolls, fruitcakes and sponge cakes to the feast. As most

**Left** *A traditional ceremonial wedding feast laid out before a newly-married Hindu couple.*

Eurasians are Catholic, they attend midnight mass on Christmas Eve and return home to the table laden with the festive delicacies.

## Chinese New Year

Shortly after Christmas, preparations for the Chinese New Year begin. Traditionally, this festival marked the advent of spring for the Chinese farmers, but for the largely urban Chinese population the event represents a spiritual renewal rather than a physical one. To clear the way for the New Year, houses are cleaned, debts settled, new clothes bought and gifts of money exchanged. On New Year's Day, orange segments are presented to guests for good fortune, and sweets (candy) and cakes are offered to ensure a sweet future.

In Malaysia, a Peranakan New Year meal usually includes chicken cooked in a tamarind sauce. In Singapore, on the seventh day of the New Year, Chinese families eat *yu sheng*, a salad of finely sliced raw fish, tossed with shredded vegetables, candied melon, pomelo segments, strips of jellyfish, peanuts, sesame seeds and lime juice, which they believe will bring them prosperity.

## Hari Raya Puasa

The third major festival on the calendar is the Muslim *Hari Raya Puasa*, which marks the end of Ramadan, the month of fasting and abstaining from other sensory pleasures between dawn and dusk. For the men, the day begins with prayers in the mosques and then they go on to the cemeteries to pay respects

to dead relatives. The women prepare the feast at home, making *rendang*, beef cooked in coconut milk, which is served with *ketupat*, compressed rice cakes, and *serunding*, a side dish of grated coconut fried with chilli. Once the meal has been consumed, friends and family visit one another, bearing gifts of cooked food, cakes and sweetmeats, which are enjoyed with endless cups of tea and coffee, or syrupy drinks.

## Diwali

The Festival of Lights, *Diwali*, is a Hindu celebration, marking the triumph of good over evil. It takes place on the rising of the new moon on the seventh month of the Hindu calendar, when oil lamps and candles are lit to welcome Lakshmi, the goddess of wealth. To

celebrate the occasion, a wonderful array of spicy *vindaloo* and *biryani* dishes, flatbreads and chutneys are prepared for friends and relatives.

## Gawai Dayak Festival

In Sarawak, the Dayaks celebrate the end of the rice harvest with a week-long festival, Gawai Dayak. The Iban and Bidayah communities also celebrate this festival, which involves a great deal of merry-making and dancing, enhanced by the home-brewed rice wine, *tuak*. Cockfights, war dances and blow pipe competitions are all part of the festivities, which are rounded off with local delicacies, such as fermented fish stir-fried with black beans, *ikan kasam*, and a touch more alcohol in the fermented durian pulp, *tempoyak*.

# Kitchens & equipment

Traditionally, cooking was regarded as a craft, passed down from generation to generation. Each culture maintained its own culinary traditions, learning through observation rather than recipes and measurements. A woman's ability to cook often determined her desirability as a wife. This was particularly so among the Peranakan communities, where the women spent a great deal of time in the kitchen, shaping the creative Nonya cuisine that is so highly thought of today.

In most parts of Malaysia, particularly in the *kampung*, food remains central to home life but, in the high-density, fast-paced living of Singapore and Kuala Lumpur, kitchens are small and meals are often bought at hawker stalls. Generally, throughout Malaysia and Singapore, the cooking and serving of food is a relaxed affair, the only rule being that the dishes must be spicy and, preferably, fiery or served with extra chillies on the side.

In most homes and restaurants, forks, spoons and chopsticks are all available, depending on your preference. In Indian and Malay households, the right hand is always used to give, receive and eat food, using flatbread as a scoop; the left hand is considered unclean. The right hand must also be kept clean to greet others in the ritual salaam, by

**Below** *A street hawker prepares a snack on his* halp *– a bamboo pole with baskets for carrying ingredients, cooking equipment and a brazier.*

**Left** *The versatile wok can be used for deep-frying and blanching as well as stir-frying and steaming.*

shredding and crushing. Peranakan cooks often add a *parut* to their kitchen utensils, which they use for grating coconut, and a special grinding stone, *batu giling*, for spices. In the Malay, Indian and Peranakan kitchen the most important utensil of all is a large, solid stone mortar and pestle, which is used for grinding and pounding wet and dry spices to make the essential spice pastes.

## Traditional pots
The Chinese and Peranakans also use clay pots for braising, and Indians often use copper pots for curries and cast-iron griddles, *tawa*, for cooking their numerous flatbreads, such as *roti paratha* and *chapati*. To treat clay pots before use, they should be filled with cold water, which is brought slowly to the boil, then simmered for 5–10 minutes and left to cool before pouring away. The pot can then go directly on the hob or stove or in the oven.

shaking hands and then raising the fingers to touch your heart. As a number of dishes, particularly the grilled and fried ones at hawker stalls, require the use of hands, finger bowls are often present at tables and stalls. Eating with the hands is common practice, but only the fingertips are used.

Elders are always greeted and treated with great respect, and served first at the table. Within each culture, hospitality is of vital importance, and the primary welcoming gesture is to offer food. And when visiting a home, it is customary to take with you a gift of fruit or sweets (candy).

## Malaysian kitchens
Kitchens are generally basic. Most households have no fancy equipment, other than perhaps a practical, modern rice steamer. For cooking, the Chinese and Malays use a wok, *kuali*, more than any other piece of equipment. The cast-iron woks are regarded as far superior and require seasoning with oil over a high heat before use. The more

you use a wok, the more seasoned it becomes, as long as you only rinse and wipe the surface clean, rather than scrubbing it in soapy water which causes it to rust.

Woks are used for stir-fried and deep-fried dishes, and a long-handled spatula, or wooden spoon, is required for tossing the ingredients quickly in the wok. Perforated ladles are used for deep-frying and blanching, and bamboo baskets, sometimes stacked in multiple layers, are designed to fit neatly inside woks, for steaming rice, fish and savoury snacks wrapped in banana leaves. In effect, apart from grilling (broiling), which is traditionally done over charcoal, most Chinese, Malay and Peranakan cooking methods can be achieved in a wok and a bamboo steamer.

Wooden chopping boards and Chinese or Japanese cleavers are essential for chopping, slicing,

**Right** *Bamboo steamers can be used singly or stacked in the wok.*

# Store-cupboard ingredients

The air in some sections of the markets is heady with the odours of the herb and spice stalls. The Malay and Peranakan herb stalls include pungent roots like ginger, galangal, lemon grass stalks, wild fern fronds, ginger buds, and betel leaves for chewing. Equally alluring are the warm aromas from the Indian spice stalls, composed of cinnamon bark, star anise, fennel and cumin seeds, cardamom pods, cloves, ground turmeric and roasted curry powders. Other stalls are laden with dried goods, oils and condiments.

Most kitchens have a supply of frequently used dried goods, seasonings, flavourings and condiments, such as candlenuts, cans of coconut milk, dried red chillies, packets of dried shrimp and the pungent shrimp paste, *belacan*, palm sugar, tamarind pulp, rice, dried egg noodles and a collection of spices, *bambu*. Chinese kitchens also keep stocks of canned bamboo shoots and water chestnuts, dried shiitake mushrooms, salted duck eggs, Chinese cooking wine, called *shao shing*, Sichuan pepper, Chinese five-spice powder and bottles of hoisin sauce, which is made from salted soya beans, sugar, vinegar, sesame oil and spices.

Chilli sauce, soy sauces, sesame or groundnut (peanut) oil, and oyster sauce are stocked in most kitchens, while garlic, shallots, ginger, lemon grass, pandanus leaves, fresh coriander (cilantro) and fresh chillies are bought regularly from the markets.

Locally produced tomato ketchup appears in sauces for deep-fried seafood, sweet and sour dishes, Singapore chilli crab, and the Malay and Indian noodle dish, *mee goreng*. Hawkers liberally use tomato ketchup to flavour everything from Chinese noodles to Western-style fast food. Another versatile condiment is *kecap manis*, which is a thick soy sauce,

sweetened with palm sugar, and used in the noodle dish, *char kway teow*, and in the filling for *popiah*.

Coconut also plays a key role. The freshly grated flesh appears in many dishes and the extracted water is used for braising and marinating. Most important, the fresh milk and cream extracted from the pulp are an integral part of many soups, noodle and rice dishes, curries and desserts.

### Chillies galore

It is impossible to imagine a meal in Malaysia or Singapore without chillies. Pounded with other spices, using a mortar and pestle, chillies play a star part in the spice paste, *rempah*, which forms an integral part of Malay and Peranakan curries. As the Malays and Peranakans enjoy their food with a fiery blast, chillies are often added as a garnish, or as a side dish, to munch on while enjoying the already fiery curry or soupy noodles. Red chillies add heat and colour to a dish, whereas the green chillies tend to be sliced on the side or pickled. Apart from adding a punch to most dishes, chillies form the basis of

**Left** *Bowls of chillies, which are often crunched on during a meal.*
**Far left** *Fragrant lemon grass stalks tied together in bundles.*

most *sambals*, which the Malays and Peranakans couldn't live without. Bird's eye chillies, *cili padi*, burn the tongue and throat the most, bringing tears to the eyes. If a Malay describes a girl as *cili padi*, he means that she packs a mighty punch and shouldn't be messed with! Dried red chillies lack the pungency of fresh ones, but retain the heat and colour. Often, they are soaked in water until soft and pounded to a paste before being added to sauces and marinades. Chilli oil, which is made by infusing dried chillies in a base oil, is drizzled over noodles, eggs and grilled and fried dishes.

*Rempah* is the heart and soul of Malay curries, soups and noodle dishes. It is also the foundation of many Nonya and Peranakan dishes. Best prepared using a solid mortar and pestle, wet ingredients such as shallots, garlic, fresh ginger and turmeric, lemon grass stalks and chillies are pounded to a paste, followed by dry spices such as cinnamon, coriander seeds, cumin and candlenuts. This spice paste, *rempah*, is then stir-fried in oil to release the natural oils and fragrance before adding the other ingredients. It performs the essential function of giving the dish a rich depth of flavour, as well as thickening the sauce.

## Sambal relish

A ubiquitous term in Malay, Peranakan and Indonesian food is *sambal*, which covers a wide range of relish-style side dishes and condiments. Some sambals are cooked, others are raw, but all are spicy and, usually, fiery with a generous helping of chopped or pounded chillies.

At its simplest *sambal ulek* is a combination of pounded chillies, vinegar and salt, which is served with a squirt of lime as a condiment for Hokkien noodles, *laksa* dishes and *nasi lemak*, Malay coconut rice.

The Malays and Peranakans serve *sambal belacan*, a mixture of pounded chillies and shrimp paste, with almost everything. *Sambal goreng* is a mixture of chillies and spices fried together to form the basis of a spicy dish, such as the popular hawker dish, *sambal goreng cumi-cumi,* squid cooked in fried *sambal.* Eurasians enjoy *sambal cili taucheo,*

made with onions and preserved soya beans, which they spoon over pan-fried fish or tofu, and the Malays insist on eating *nasi lemak* with *sambal ikan bilis*, dried anchovies fried with sambal. For the Malays and Indonesians, *bumbu saté* or *sambal kacang* are both names of the same traditional chilli and peanut dipping sauce that is served with satay and other grilled meats. As *sambals* form such an integral part of the Malay cuisine, they even crop up in other parts of the world, such as South Africa, where the Cape Malays have transported their favourite condiment.

# Broths & soupy noodles

# Broths & soupy noodles

Throughout South-east Asia, soups and broths are designed to cleanse the mouth and refresh the palate. In Malaysia and Singapore, where the predominant cultures are Malay and Chinese, the light, clear broths perform this role, but many of the heavier soups are served in the home, or from the hawker stalls, as meals on their own with bread or rice. Soupy noodles may be enjoyed as a snack or as a main dish, served with bread on the side.

Bowls of steaming broth are often served alongside the main course, so that diners can slurp a spoonful of soup in between spoonfuls of rice or the main dish. These broths are also appreciated as "wet" dishes, the idea being that a little is spooned over the accompanying bowl of steamed rice to moisten it. Some of the heavier Eurasian and Indian soups are served as meals on their own, at any time of day. The spicy Indian mutton soup, *sop kambing*, is regarded as an effective pick-me-up late at night. Similarly, the traditional, aromatic pork bone tea, *bak kut teh*, is valued for its restorative properties, whether it is taken early in the morning or late at night.

## Chinese-style soups

A traditional dish that features in the Chinese kitchen is the soup made with sharks' fins. Nowadays, it is an expensive soup to make and correspondingly pricey in restaurants. Not only are the sharks heavily over-fished and consequently rare, but also the fins themselves have great value. High in protein and believed to contain medicinal properties, sharks' fins are dried and sold in Chinese markets and medicine shops. The shredded fins are considered poor in quality, whereas the whole dried fins are much sought after but require a great deal of preparation.

First the whole fin needs 4–5 hours of simmering in multiple changes of water, until the skin can be peeled off and the bone removed. The fin flesh is then simmered for a further 5 hours in a broth, until it is tender and gelatinous. For the Chinese, this time-consuming preparation and the shark's rarity add to the soup's attraction and prestige. For others, shark's fin soup is best left to ponder over.

Chinese noodle soups and soupy noodles have long been a tradition of the hawker stalls and are very popular in the food centres and coffee shops.

**Left** *Simmering the shark's fin in a cauldron of water to make soup.*

**Right** *Fresh coriander (cilantro) leaves are used in many Malaysian dishes.* **Far right** *Noodles are often sold in bundles in the markets.*

Traditionally, the soups are clear, containing noodles in the broth, whereas the soupy noodles consist of noodles and other ingredients in a liquid coconut milk sauce, resulting in a dish that could be served as a soup or a main course. Generally, soupy noodles are served on their own with bread to mop up all the tasty sauce.

## Laksa

One of the most interesting dishes in Malaysia and Singapore is *laksa*. Consisting primarily of noodles in spicy coconut milk, it represents the meeting point of the Chinese and Malay culinary cultures. However, there are as many versions of *laksa* as there are regions in Malaysia. The thick *laksa* from Kedah uses dried slices of tamarind and is garnished with strips of cucumber and onion; the rich *laksa* from Johor includes mackerel or herring and Indian spices such as cumin, coriander and turmeric; the sour Penang *laksa* is made with blocks of tamarind and flakes of fish, and garnished with pineapple; Ipoh *laksa* resembles a curry with the addition of grilled pork; Sarawak *laksa* has an interesting depth of colour and flavour from the roasted rice and coconut, which is tweaked with bitter-sweet kalamansi lime; and the popular, creamy Singapore *laksa*, created by the Nonya women, is supreme in its balance of Chinese and Malay cooking styles.

When cooking at home, all the soups and soupy noodles in this section can be treated as meals on their own, with chunks of fresh, crusty bread, or in smaller portions as a first course.

With the food stalls and coffee shops producing delicious soups and snacks all day long, there are no hard and fast rules, other than that pleasure should be derived from eating.

**Left** *Singapore* laksa *cooked by the Nonyas represents the best of Chinese and Malay cooking.*

**Serves four to six**

### For the stock

45ml/3 tbsp dried shrimp

1 dried red chilli

50g/2oz fresh root ginger, peeled and sliced

2 onions, quartered

4 cloves garlic, bruised

2 lemon grass stalks, bruised

2.5ml/$\frac{1}{2}$ tsp black peppercorns

30–45ml/2–3 tbsp dark soy sauce

700g/1lb 10oz pork and chicken bones

### For the soup

15ml/1 tbsp sugar

6 rashers (strips) streaky (fatty) bacon, sliced

150g/5oz fresh egg noodles

20 fresh, large prawns (shrimp), peeled (add the shells to the stock)

90g/3$\frac{1}{2}$oz beansprouts

2 spring onions (scallions), trimmed and finely sliced

salt and ground black pepper

# Hokkein prawn noodle soup

Introduced to Malaysia and Singapore by the Chinese from Fujian, Hokkein noodle soup, *hay mee*, is sold at the hawker stalls, and in the coffee shops. As most of the Chinese population of Singapore is Hokkein, it is a very popular dish. Traditionally, prawn noodle soup is served with crispy cubes of pork fat, but in this recipe, crispy bacon is used instead.

**1** Put all the stock ingredients into a deep pan along with the prawn shells. Pour in 2 litres/3$\frac{1}{2}$ pints/7$\frac{3}{4}$ cups water and bring to the boil. Reduce the heat and simmer gently, uncovered, for about 2 hours, until the stock has reduced by half.

**2** Strain the stock into a clean pan and put it over a low heat to keep hot. Season with salt and pepper to taste.

**3** In a small pan heat the sugar with 15ml/1 tbsp water, until it turns a rich brown. Add it to the stock and mix well. In a heavy pan, dry-fry the bacon until it turns crispy and golden. Drain on kitchen paper and set aside.

**4** Using a perforated ladle or sieve (strainer), plunge the noodles into the hot stock for 1 minute to heat through, then divide them among four bowls. Add the prawns to the stock, heat for 1 minute, remove with a slotted spoon and add to the bowls. Add the beansprouts to the prawns and noodles and ladle the hot stock into the bowls. Scatter the crispy bacon and spring onions over the top and serve immediately.

**Per Portion** Energy 257Kcal/1082kJ; Protein 18.7g; Carbohydrate 27.1g, of which sugars 6.9g; Fat 9g, of which saturates 2.8g; Cholesterol 94mg; Calcium 145mg; Fibre 3g; Sodium 1080mg.

**Serves four**

30ml/2 tbsp vegetable oil

15–30ml/1–2 tbsp tamarind paste

15ml/1 tbsp sugar

450g/1lb fresh prawns (shrimp), peeled and deveined

4 thick fresh pineapple slices, cored and cut into bitesize chunks

salt and ground black pepper

fresh coriander (cilantro) and mint leaves, to garnish

steamed rice or plain noodles, to serve

**For the spice paste**

4 shallots, chopped

4 red chillies, chopped

25g/1oz fresh root ginger, peeled and chopped

1 lemon grass stalk, trimmed and chopped

5ml/1 tsp shrimp paste

# Singapore hot and sour pineapple prawn broth

This simple Nonya dish is served as an appetite enhancer because of its hot and sour flavour. It is also popular as an accompaniment to plain rice or noodles. In some restaurants, the broth is presented in a hollowed-out pineapple, halved lengthways.

**1** Using a mortar and pestle or a food processor, grind the shallots, chillies, ginger and lemon grass to a paste. Add the shrimp paste and mix well.

**2** Heat the oil in a wok or heavy pan. Stir in the spice paste and fry until fragrant. Stir in the tamarind paste and the sugar, then pour in 1.2 litres/2 pints/5 cups water. Mix well and bring to the boil. Reduce the heat and simmer for 10 minutes. Season the broth with salt and pepper.

**3** Add the prawns and pineapple to the broth and simmer for 4–5 minutes, or until the prawns are cooked. Using a slotted spoon, lift the prawns and pineapple out of the broth and divide them among four warmed bowls. Ladle over some of the broth and garnish with coriander and mint leaves. The remaining broth can be served separately as a drink, or spooned over steamed rice or plain noodles, if they are accompanying this dish.

**Per Portion** Energy 192Kcal/808kJ; Protein 20.4g; Carbohydrate 14.2g, of which sugars 13.9g; Fat 6.4g, of which saturates 0.8g; Cholesterol 219mg; Calcium 111mg; Fibre 1.3g; Sodium 216mg.

# Chinese fish ball soup

**Serves four to six**

**For the fish balls**

450g/1lb fresh fish fillets (such as haddock, cod, whiting or bream), boned and flaked

15–30ml/1–2 tbsp rice flour

salt and ground black pepper

**For the soup**

1.5 litres/2½ pints/6¼ cups fish or chicken stock

15–30ml/1–2 tbsp light soy sauce

4–6 mustard green leaves, chopped

90g/3½oz mung bean thread noodles, soaked in hot water until soft

**For the garnish**

2 spring onions (scallions), trimmed and finely sliced

1 red or green chilli, seeded and finely sliced

fresh coriander (cilantro) leaves, finely chopped

This light Chinese soup can be found in coffee shops and at the *tze char* stalls, where the food is ordered from the menu and cooked on the spot. Often eaten as a snack or light lunch, the soup is garnished with spring onions and fresh chillies, and the Malays often add an extra drizzle of chilli sauce or a dollop of chilli *sambal*.

**1** To make the fish balls, grind the flaked flesh to a paste, using a mortar and pestle or food processor. Season with salt and pepper and stir in 60ml/4 tbsp water. Add enough rice flour to form a paste. Take small portions of fish paste into your hands and squeeze them to mould into balls.

**2** Meanwhile, bring the stock to the boil in a deep pan and season to taste with soy sauce. Drop in the fish balls and simmer for 5 minutes. Add the shredded mustard greens and cook for 1 minute.

**3** Divide the noodles among four to six bowls. Using a slotted spoon, add the fish balls and greens to the noodles, then ladle over the hot stock. Garnish with the spring onions and chilli and sprinkle the chopped coriander over the top.

**Per Portion** Energy 127Kcal/533kJ; Protein 14.9g; Carbohydrate 14.8g, of which sugars 0.5g; Fat 0.6g, of which saturates 0.1g; Cholesterol 35mg; Calcium 17mg; Fibre 0.2g; Sodium 408mg.

# Hot and sour fish soup

*Ikan asam pedas* is the Malay version of the hot and sour fish soup found throughout South-east Asia. The sour notes are derived from the use of tamarind, whereas the hot flavourings come from the chilli-based *rempah*, the foundation of many Malaysian soups and curries. The Peranakans also have their own version of this hot and sour fish soup, which they serve with steamed rice. Generally, the Malays eat it with chunks of bread to dip into the highly flavoured broth.

**1** To make the *rempah*, grind all the ingredients to a paste, using a mortar and pestle or food processor.

**2** Heat the oil in a wok or heavy pan, and stir in the *rempah*. Fry it until it is fragrant and begins to change colour. Stir in the tamarind paste and add the snake beans, tossing them around the wok until they are coated in the spice mixture.

**3** Pour in 900ml/1½ pints/3¾ cups water and bring to the boil. Reduce the heat and simmer for 5 minutes. Season with salt and pepper, then add the fish cutlets. Cook gently for 2–3 minutes until cooked through, then ladle the soup into bowls. Garnish with coriander and serve with steamed rice or chunks of fresh bread.

### Serves four

30ml/2 tbsp vegetable oil

15–30ml/1–2 tbsp tamarind paste

115g/4oz snake beans (long beans), trimmed

450g/1lb fish cutlets (such as trout, cod, sea perch, pike), about 2.5cm/1in thick

fresh coriander (cilantro) leaves, to garnish

rice or bread, to serve

### For the *rempah*

8 dried red chillies, soaked in warm water until soft, drained and seeded

8 shallots, chopped

4 garlic cloves, chopped

2 lemon grass stalks, trimmed and sliced

25g/1oz fresh galangal, chopped

25g/1oz fresh turmeric, chopped

5ml/1 tsp shrimp paste

**Per Portion** Energy 164Kcal/686kJ; Protein 21.7g; Carbohydrate 4.9g, of which sugars 3.5g; Fat 6.5g, of which saturates 0.8g; Cholesterol 52mg; Calcium 33mg; Fibre 1.3g; Sodium 69mg.

# Noodles in spicy tangy soup

This classic Nonya dish, *mee siam*, has been influenced by the flavourings of neighbouring Thailand, with the sour notes emanating from the tamarind and salted soya beans. Almost every food stall has its own version of *mee siam*, which has been adapted to suit Malay, Chinese and Indian tastes. Salted soya beans and tamarind paste are available in Chinese and Asian stores, and in some supermarkets.

**Serves four**

vegetable oil, for deep-frying

225g/8oz firm tofu, rinsed, drained and cut into cubes

60ml/4 tbsp dried prawns (shrimp), soaked until rehydrated

5ml/1 tsp shrimp paste

4 garlic cloves, chopped

4–6 dried red chillies, soaked to soften, drained, seeded and the pulp scraped out

90g/3½oz/¾ cup roasted peanuts, ground

50g/2oz salted soya beans

2 lemon grass stalks, trimmed, halved and bruised

30ml/2 tbsp sugar

15–30ml/1–2 tbsp tamarind paste

150g/5oz dried rice vermicelli, soaked in hot water until pliable

a handful of beansprouts, rinsed and drained

4 quail's eggs, hard-boiled, shelled and halved

2 spring onions (scallions), finely sliced

salt and ground black pepper

fresh coriander (cilantro) leaves, finely chopped, to garnish

**1** In a wok, heat enough vegetable oil for deep-frying. Drop in the tofu and deep-fry until golden. Drain on kitchen paper and set aside.

**2** Using a mortar and pestle or food processor, grind the soaked dried prawns with the shrimp paste, garlic and chilli pulp to form a paste.

**3** Heat 30ml/2 tbsp of vegetable oil in a wok and stir in the paste. Fry for 1 minute until fragrant, then add the peanuts, salted soya beans and lemon grass. Fry for another minute and stir in the sugar and tamarind paste, followed by 900ml/1½ pints/3¾ cups water. Mix well and bring to the boil. Reduce the heat and simmer gently for 10 minutes. Season with salt and pepper.

**4** Drain the noodles and, using a sieve (strainer) or perforated ladle, plunge the noodles into the broth to heat through. Divide the noodles among individual serving bowls, sprinkle over the beansprouts and add the deep-fried tofu, halved quail's eggs and spring onions. Ladle the spicy broth over the top, garnish with the coriander and serve immediately.

**Cook's tip** This is such a tasty, spicy dish that it is best served on its own as a light meal or nourishing snack so that the flavours can be fully appreciated.

Per Portion Energy 547Kcal/2280kJ; Protein 29.5g; Carbohydrate 42.5g, of which sugars 10g; Fat 29g, of which saturates 4.4g; Cholesterol 48mg; Calcium 389mg; Fibre 3.7g; Sodium 203mg.

# Singapore *laksa*

There are as many *laksa* dishes as there are diverse regions in Malaysia and Singapore. The basic dish consists of noodles in a spicy coconut broth. In the home-cooked Singapore *laksa*, slices of deep-fried fish cakes are often added at the end, whereas the stall version is rich in a variety of seafood, topped with cockles.

**1** Using a mortar and pestle or food processor, grind all the ingredients for the spice paste mixture, apart from the oil. Bind the paste with the oil and set aside.

**2** Heat enough oil in a wok to deep-fry. Add the shallots to the oil and deep-fry until crispy and golden. Drain and set aside.

**3** Heat 30ml/2 tbsp vegetable oil in a large wok or heavy pan. Stir in the spice paste and cook over a low heat for 3–4 minutes, until fragrant. Add the coconut milk and chicken stock and bring to the boil, stirring all the time. Add the prawns, squid and scallops and simmer gently, for about 5–10 minutes, until cooked. Add the cockles at the last minute and season the broth with salt and pepper.

**4** Ladle the noodles into individual bowls. Add the beansprouts and ladle over the broth and seafood, making sure the noodles are submerged in the steaming liquid. Garnish with the crispy shallots, mint and a drizzle of chilli oil.

**Serves four to six**

**For the spice paste**

8 shallots, chopped

4 garlic cloves, chopped

40g/1½oz fresh root ginger, peeled and chopped

2 lemon grass stalks, chopped

6 candlenuts or macadamia nuts

4 dried red chillies, soaked until soft and seeded

30ml/2 tbsp dried prawns (shrimp), soaked until soft

5–10ml/1–2 tsp *belacan*

5–10ml/1–2 tsp sugar

15ml/1 tbsp vegetable oil

**For the *laksa***

vegetable oil, for deep-frying

6 shallots, finely sliced

600ml/1 pint/2½ cups coconut milk

400ml/14fl oz/1⅔ cups chicken stock

90g/3½oz prawns (shrimp), shelled

90g/3½oz squid, cleaned, trimmed and sliced

6–8 scallops

75g/3oz cockles, shelled

225g/8oz fresh rice noodles or dried rice vermicelli, soaked in lukewarm water until pliable

90g/3½oz beansprouts

salt and ground black pepper

a small bunch of Vietnamese mint or fresh garden mint, roughly chopped, and chilli oil, to garnish

**Per Portion** Energy 300Kcal/1254kJ; Protein 14.2g; Carbohydrate 38g, of which sugars 6.9g; Fat 10.3g, of which saturates 1.4g; Cholesterol 77mg; Calcium 69mg; Fibre 0.7g; Sodium 211mg.

# Eurasian curried soup

With a culinary culture born from Indian, Malay, Chinese and European traditions, the Eurasians have some distinct dishes of their own. As they trace their roots to Malaka during the Portuguese and Dutch periods, many of the dishes are linked to that region and employ Portuguese methods, such as cooking in earthenware pots. Chicken feet are sometimes added to the stock in this recipe to enrich it.

**1** To make the curry paste, grind the ginger with the garlic, shallots and lemon grass, using a mortar and pestle or food processor. Add the chilli pulp and curry powder and set aside.

**2** Put the chicken and the chicken feet, if using, in a deep pan with the cinnamon sticks, peppercorns, fennel and cumin seeds. Add enough water to just cover, and bring it to the boil. Reduce the heat and cook gently for about 1 hour, until the chicken is cooked. Remove the chicken from the broth, skin it and shred the meat. Strain the broth.

**3** In an earthenware pot or wok, heat the ghee or oil. Stir in the mustard seeds and, once they begin to pop and give off a nutty aroma, add the curry paste. Fry the paste until fragrant, then pour in the strained broth. Bring the broth to the boil and season to taste with salt and pepper. Add the curry leaves and shredded chicken, and ladle the soup into bowls. Serve with wedges of lime to squeeze into the soup.

### Serves four to six

1 chicken, about 1kg/2¼lb

2 chicken feet (optional)

2 cinnamon sticks

5ml/1 tsp black peppercorns

5ml/1 tsp fennel seeds

5ml/1 tsp cumin seeds

15 ml/1 tbsp ghee or vegetable oil with a little butter

15–30ml/1–2 tbsp brown mustard seeds

a handful of fresh curry leaves

salt and ground black pepper

2 limes, quartered, to serve

### For the curry paste

40g/1½oz fresh root ginger, peeled and chopped

4 garlic cloves, chopped

4 shallots, chopped

2 lemon grass stalks, trimmed and chopped

4 dried red chillies, soaked to soften, drained, seeded and the pulp scraped out

15–30ml/1–2 tbsp Indian curry powder

**Per Portion** Energy 264Kcal/1093kJ; Protein 20.7g; Carbohydrate 1.6g, of which sugars 1g; Fat 19.4g, of which saturates 6.3g; Cholesterol 112mg; Calcium 19mg; Fibre 0.5g; Sodium 104mg.

**Serves six**

1 small chicken, about 900g/2lb

2 lemon grass stalks, bruised

25g/1oz fresh root ginger, peeled and sliced

2 fresh kaffir lime leaves

1 dried red chilli

30ml/2 tbsp vegetable oil

50g/2oz mung bean thread noodles, soaked until pliable

3 hard-boiled eggs, peeled and halved

115g/4oz beansprouts

a small bunch of fresh coriander (cilantro), roughly chopped, to garnish

2 limes, quartered, chilli oil and soy sauce, to serve

**For the *rempah***

8 shallots, chopped

8 garlic cloves, chopped

6 candlenuts or macadamia nuts

50g/2oz galangal, chopped

2 lemon grass stalks, chopped

4 fresh kaffir lime leaves

15ml/1 tbsp ground coriander

10ml/2 tsp ground turmeric

15ml/1 tbsp vegetable oil

# Spicy chicken soup

This fragrant soup, *soto ayam*, is particularly popular in Singapore. Originally from Java, various versions are served at soup and noodle stalls specializing in Indonesian and Malay food. As many Malay Singaporeans came from Indonesia, it is always in demand. When served as a meal on its own, deep-fried potato fritters or chips (French fries), or the Malay compressed rice cakes, *ketupat*, are added to the soup.

**1** Using a mortar and pestle or a food processor, grind all the *rempah* ingredients to a paste. Set aside.

**2** Put the chicken, lemon grass, ginger, lime leaves and chilli into a deep pan and pour in enough water to just cover. Bring to the boil, reduce the heat, cover and simmer for about 1 hour, until the chicken is tender. Remove the chicken from the stock, take off and discard the skin and tear the meat into shreds. Strain the stock.

**3** In a wok or heavy pan, heat the oil. Stir in the *rempah* and cook for 1–2 minutes, until fragrant. Pour in the stock and stir well. Season to taste with salt and pepper.

**4** Divide the noodles among six bowls. Add the hard-boiled eggs, beansprouts and shredded chicken. Ladle the steaming broth into each bowl and garnish with coriander. Serve immediately with the lime wedges, chilli oil and soy sauce to squeeze, drizzle and pour over it.

**Per Portion** Energy 493Kcal/2050kJ; Protein 36g; Carbohydrate 8.5g, of which sugars 1g; Fat 35.1g, of which saturates 9.1g; Cholesterol 258mg; Calcium 47mg; Fibre 0.8g; Sodium 178mg.

## Serves four to six

25g/1oz fresh root ginger, peeled and chopped

4–6 garlic cloves, chopped

1 red chilli, seeded and chopped

15ml/1 tbsp ghee or vegetable oil

5ml/1 tsp coriander seeds

5ml/1 tsp cumin seeds

5ml/1 tsp ground fenugreek

5ml/1 tsp sugar

450g/1lb meaty mutton ribs, cut into bitesize pieces

2 litres/3½ pints/7¾ cups lamb stock or water

10ml/2 tsp tomato purée (paste)

1 cinnamon stick

4–6 cardamom pods, bruised

2 tomatoes, peeled and quartered

salt and ground black pepper

fresh coriander (cilantro) leaves, roughly chopped, to garnish

# Indian mutton soup

*Sop kambing* is a popular dish at the Muslim and Malay hawker stalls as well as in the coffee shops. It is a soup that comes into its own late at night, when it is valued for its restorative qualities. It also makes a great supper dish, served with chunks of crusty bread or Indian flatbread.

**1** Using a mortar and pestle or a food processor, grind the ginger, garlic and chilli to a paste.

**2** Heat the ghee or oil in a heavy pan and stir in the coriander and cumin seeds. Add the ginger, garlic and chilli paste along with the fenugreek and sugar. Stir until fragrant and beginning to colour. Add the chopped mutton ribs, searing the meat on both sides.

**3** Pour in the stock or water and stir in the tomato purée, cinnamon stick and cardamom pods. Bring to the boil, then reduce the heat, cover the pan and simmer gently for 1½ hours, until the meat is very tender.

**4** Season to taste with salt and pepper. Stir in the tomatoes, and garnish with coriander. Serve hot with chunks of fresh crusty bread or Indian flatbread.

**Per Portion** Energy 166Kcal/693kJ; Protein 15.2g; Carbohydrate 2.8g, of which sugars 2.5g; Fat 10.6g, of which saturates 5.2g; Cholesterol 62mg; Calcium 12mg; Fibre 0.5g; Sodium 87mg.

# Pork bone tea

The literal translation of *bak kut teh*, pork bone tea, doesn't do justice to this aromatic, peppery broth made from pork ribs and sometimes the internal organs of the pig. It is a favourite at the late-night hawker stalls and in the coffee shops, where it is particularly popular with the older folk, who sip it when they gather for a chat. The broth is served with bowls of steamed white rice, and the tender pork flesh is dipped into soy sauce infused with chillies.

**1** To make the dipping sauce, stir the soy sauce and chillies together in a small bowl and set aside. To make the spice bag, lay the piece of muslin flat and place all the spices in the centre. Gather up the edges and tie together to form a bag.

**2** Put the pork ribs and loin into a deep pan. Add the garlic, cinnamon sticks, star anise and spice bag. Pour in 2.5 litres/4½ pints/10 cups water and bring to the boil.

**3** Skim off any fat from the surface, then stir in the soy sauces and sugar. Reduce the heat and simmer, partially covered, for about 2 hours, until the pork is almost falling off the bones. Season to taste with salt and lots of black pepper.

**4** Remove the loin from the broth and cut it into bitesize pieces. Divide the meat and ribs among four to six bowls and ladle the steaming broth over the top. Serve with the soy and chilli sauce, as a dip for the pieces of pork, and steamed rice.

### Serves four to six

500g/1¼lb meaty pork ribs, trimmed and cut into 5cm/2in lengths

225g/8oz pork loin

8 garlic cloves, unpeeled and bruised

2 cinnamon sticks

5 star anise

120ml/4fl oz/½ cup light soy sauce

50ml/2fl oz/¼ cup dark soy sauce

15ml/1 tbsp sugar

salt and ground black pepper

steamed rice, to serve

### For the dipping sauce

120ml/4fl oz/½ cup light soy sauce

2 red chillies, seeded and finely chopped

### For the spice bag

6 cloves

15ml/1 tbsp dried orange peel

5ml/1 tsp black peppercorns

5ml/1 tsp coriander seeds

5ml/1 tsp fennel seeds

a piece of muslin (cheesecloth)

**Per Portion** Energy 49Kcal/206kJ; Protein 8.1g; Carbohydrate 0.8g, of which sugars 0.8g; Fat 1.5g, of which saturates 0.5g; Cholesterol 24mg; Calcium 3mg; Fibre 0g; Sodium 145mg.

# Fried & grilled snacks

# Fried & grilled snacks

Snacking is a great Malay and Chinese tradition. At times it seems as if the locals never stop nibbling. With such an emphasis on hawker stalls and food centres, there are always delicious cooking odours enticing you to stop and have a little bite to eat. Very often these snacks will be grilled or deep-fried, the simplest methods of cooking at a stall. Street stalls still exist in Malaysia but in Singapore most of them have been rehoused indoors in large food centres.

In many places, street stalls have established a long tradition, and they often produce some of the most delicious food around. The Muslim and Malay stalls, which are often grouped together, produce a wonderful mix of rice and noodle dishes served with fried and grilled accompaniments, such as chargrilled or fried prawns (shrimp), scallops and squid; fried lentil patties; eggs in a tangy sauce; fried dried anchovies, *ikan bilis goreng*, which the Malays and Peranakans love with *nasi lemak*, coconut rice; and *epok-epok*, triangular pastries filled with spicy vegetables or meat, which could be described as a Malay version of the well-known Indian *samosa*. These stalls also offer fried sweet snacks, such as deep-fried bananas in coconut batter, sprinkled with sugar.

At the grill stalls, which are easily identified by the enticing aromas that travel through the clouds of smoke, you can tuck into the tastiest spicy chicken wings, grilled stingray wings, and the ever-popular satay. A great Malay favourite, satay probably evolved from the Arab kebab, which would have been introduced to Melaka by Arab traders once Islam had taken hold of the

**Left** *A street food vendor fanning the flames at a satay stall.*

Left *Oysters make a luxurious ingredient in a sumptuous omelette.*
Far left *Fresh prawns (shrimp) are used in many Malay and Chinese dishes.*

and Indian dishes. In its many disguises, it emerges as *roti kaya*, smeared in coconut jam, and *roti telur*, with an egg cracked in the middle, or as a slight variation on the theme, *roti bawang telur*, where the egg in the middle is topped with chopped onions.

Other breads on offer include *murtabak*, which is like *roti paratha* but filled with spicy minced (ground) lamb, chicken, or vegetables, various forms of *dosai*, paper-thin crêpes made with rice and lentils, and *appam* or hoppers, the fermented rice cakes that are cooked in tiny, individual woks and served with sugar as a sweet treat.

region. With such an eclectic mix of cultures in Malaysia and Singapore, the traditional pork or chicken satay has metamorphosed into every form of seafood, vegetables, such as aubergines (eggplants) and sweet potatoes, beef, water buffalo, duck, wild boar in Sabah and mutton or goat in Sarawak. All these different kinds of satay are served with a piquant peanut or pineapple sauce or a chilli *sambal*.

## Help-yourself buffets

Another interesting place for savoury snacks is the *cze cha* stall, a kind of self-service buffet spread. Usually, a stack of bowls flank the appetizing display of tasty delights, such as stuffed chillies, fried tofu, stir-fried *kangkong* (water spinach), Chinese spring rolls, and the Nonya version, *popiah*, to which diners help themselves.

The Indian *roti* stalls and hopper stands are very popular places for

eating snacks and breakfast. The griddle-fried, flaky flatbread *roti paratha* is one of the most popular breads to accompany Malay, Nonya

Right *Sweet and sour deep-fried squid is a popular snack.*

**Serves four (makes 8 *parathas*)**

225g/8oz/2 cups plain (all-purpose) white flour or rice flour

225g/8oz/2 cups wholemeal (whole-wheat) flour

5ml/1 tsp salt

200g/7oz/scant 1 cup ghee or butter

extra flour, for dusting

# Fried Indian bread

The bread (*roti*) stalls are generally run by Indians, who expertly knead and slap the bread doughs and flick them in the air before frying them on a griddle. This recipe is for the plain, flaky flatbread *roti paratha*. It is served with curries for breakfast, lunch and supper, or is simply sprinkled with sugar for a quick sweet snack mid-morning.

**1** Sift the flours, with the salt, into a wide bowl. Make a well in the centre and pour in 300ml/½ pint/1¼ cups water, drawing the flour in from the sides. Knead the dough for about 10 minutes, then cover the bowl with a damp dishtowel and set aside for 3 hours. Put the ghee or butter into a small pan and melt it over a low heat.

**2** Knead the dough again and divide it into 8 portions, rolling each one into a ball – if the dough is too sticky, add a little extra flour while kneading. Dust a work surface with flour and, using the palm of your hand, flatten one of the balls of dough on it. Roll the dough into an 18cm/7in circle and brush it with the melted ghee.

**3** Dust a little flour over the ghee, then roll the *paratha* into a tight sausage. Wrap it around itself into a coil and place it on the floured surface.

**4** Press down on the coil with the palm of your hand to form a patty and roll it into an 18cm/7in circle again. Repeat with the other balls of dough and keep them moist under a damp dishtowel.

**5** Heat a cast-iron griddle or heavy frying pan and place one *paratha* on it. Leave it for 30 seconds, then lift it up and brush some ghee under it. Press down on the *paratha*, moving it around occasionally, for about 2 minutes, then brush some ghee on the top side and flip it over. Cook the second side for about 3 minutes, pressing down on it and moving it around occasionally – it should be nicely browned in patches.

**6** Wrap the cooked *paratha* in foil or a dry dishtowel, and repeat with the other balls of dough. They can be cooked and stacked in foil and then heated in the oven before serving. Serve with Indian and Malay curries and soups, or on their own with sugar or jam.

**Per Portion** Energy 738Kcal/3087kJ; Protein 12.7g; Carbohydrate 80g, of which sugars 2.3g; Fat 43.1g, of which saturates 26.3g; Cholesterol 107mg; Calcium 109mg; Fibre 6.8g; Sodium 798mg.

**Serves four**

vegetable oil, for deep-frying

8 eggs, hard-boiled and shelled

1 lemon grass stalk, trimmed, quartered and crushed

2 large tomatoes, skinned, seeded and chopped to a pulp

5–10ml/1–2 tsp sugar

30ml/2 tbsp dark soy sauce

juice of 1 lime

fresh coriander (cilantro) and mint leaves, coarsely chopped, to garnish

**For the *rempah***

4–6 red chillies, seeded and chopped

4 shallots, chopped

2 garlic cloves, chopped

2.5ml/½ tsp shrimp paste

# Fried hard-boiled eggs in hot red sauce

A popular snack at Malay stalls, this spicy egg dish originally came from Indonesia. Served wrapped in a banana leaf, the Malays often eat it with plain steamed rice, sliced chillies, onion and coriander – ideal for a quick, tasty snack or light lunch.

**1** Using a mortar and pestle or food processor, grind the ingredients for the *rempah* to form a smooth paste. Set aside.

**2** Heat enough oil for deep-frying in a wok or heavy pan and deep-fry the whole boiled eggs until golden brown. Lift them out and drain.

**3** Reserve 15ml/1 tbsp of the oil and discard the rest. Heat the oil in the wok or heavy pan and stir in the *rempah* until it becomes fragrant. Add the lemon grass, followed by the tomatoes and sugar. Cook for 2–3 minutes, until it forms a thick paste. Reduce the heat and stir in the soy sauce and lime juice. Add 30ml/2 tbsp water to thin the sauce. Toss in the eggs, making sure they are thoroughly coated, and serve hot, garnished with chopped coriander and mint leaves.

**Per Portion** Energy 271Kcal/1125kJ; Protein 13.3g; Carbohydrate 5.5g, of which sugars 5g; Fat 22.3g, of which saturates 4.4g; Cholesterol 381mg; Calcium 67mg; Fibre 0.7g; Sodium 679mg.

**Serves four**

4 shallots, chopped

2 garlic cloves, chopped

4 dried red chillies, soaked in warm water until soft, seeded and chopped

30ml/2 tbsp tamarind pulp, soaked in 150ml/$\frac{1}{4}$ pint/$\frac{2}{3}$ cup water until soft

vegetable oil, for deep-frying

115g/4oz/1 cup peanuts

200g/7oz dried anchovies, heads removed, washed and drained

30ml/2 tbsp sugar

bread or rice, to serve

# Fried dried anchovies with peanuts

The Malays and Peranakans love fried dried anchovies, *ikan bilis goreng*. Generally, they are served as a snack with bread or as an accompaniment to coconut rice, *nasi lemak*. The Malays also enjoy them with *bubur*, rice porridge, for breakfast.

**1** Using a mortar and pestle or food processor, grind the shallots, garlic and chillies to a coarse paste. Squeeze the tamarind pulp to help soften it in the water and press it through a sieve (strainer). Measure out 120ml/4fl oz/$\frac{1}{2}$ cup of the tamarind water.

**2** Heat enough oil for deep-frying in a wok. Lower the heat and deep-fry the peanuts in a wire basket, until they colour. Drain them on kitchen paper. Add the anchovies to the oil and deep-fry until brown and crisp. Drain the anchovies on kitchen paper.

**3** Pour out most of the oil from the wok, reserving 30ml/2 tbsp. Stir in the spice paste and fry until fragrant. Add the sugar, anchovies and peanuts. Gradually stir in the tamarind water, so the mixture remains dry. Serve hot or cold with bread or rice.

**Per Portion** Energy 338Kcal/1400kJ; Protein 17g; Carbohydrate 4.8g, of which sugars 2.6g; Fat 28g, of which saturates 4.4g; Cholesterol 24mg; Calcium 134mg; Fibre 2g; Sodium 1475mg.

# Sweet and sour deep-fried squid

A favourite at the Singapore hawker stalls, deep-fried squid served with a sweet and sour sauce is popular with the Malays, Chinese, Peranakans and Eurasians. This is an example of a dish where the Western influence comes into play – with tomato ketchup and Worcestershire sauce.

**1** First prepare the squid. Hold the body in one hand and pull off the head with the other. Sever the tentacles and discard the rest. Remove the backbone and clean the body sack inside and out. Pat dry using kitchen paper and cut into rings.

**2** In a bowl, mix the soy sauce with the sugar until it dissolves. Toss in the squid rings and tentacles and leave to marinate for 1 hour.

**3** Meanwhile prepare the sauce. Mix together the tomato ketchup, Worcestershire sauce, soy sauce and oil. Sweeten with sugar or honey to taste and add as much chilli oil as you like. Set aside.

**4** Heat enough oil for deep-frying in a wok or heavy pan. Thoroughly drain the squid of any marinade, pat with kitchen paper to avoid spitting, and fry until golden and crispy. Pat dry on kitchen paper and serve immediately with the dipping sauce.

**Serves four**

900g/2lb fresh young, tender squid

vegetable oil, for deep-frying

**For the marinade**

60ml/4 tbsp light soy sauce

15ml/1 tbsp sugar

**For the dipping sauce**

30ml/2 tbsp tomato ketchup

15ml/1 tbsp Worcestershire sauce

15ml/1 tbsp light soy sauce

15ml/1 tbsp vegetable or sesame oil

sugar or honey, to sweeten

chilli oil, to taste

**Cook's tip** To avoid the spitting fat, lightly coat the squid in flour before deep-frying. Alternatively, fry in a deep-fat fryer with a lid or use a spatterproof cover on the wok or pan.

Per Portion Energy 315Kcal/1320kJ; Protein 35.2g; Carbohydrate 4.5g, of which sugars 1.7g; Fat 17.6g, of which saturates 2.5g; Cholesterol 506mg; Calcium 39mg; Fibre 0g; Sodium 1361mg.

# Grilled tamarind prawns

This is a great favourite among the Malays, Peranakans and Indonesians. The aroma emanating from the Malay grill stalls as large, marinated prawns are grilled over charcoal makes you feel very hungry. Rather expertly, the Malaysians crunch the whole prawn, sucking in all the tamarind flavouring while spitting out the bits of shell. The marinade is seasoned and sweetened with *kecap manis*, soy sauce sweetened with palm sugar, but you could replace it with the same quantity of dark soy sauce blended with a little palm or muscovado sugar.

**Serves two to four**

500g/1¼lb fresh, large prawns (shrimp)

45ml/3 tbsp tamarind pulp

30ml/2 tbsp *kecap manis*

15ml/1 tbsp sugar

ground black pepper

fresh coriander (cilantro) leaves and 2–4 green chillies, seeded and quartered lengthways, to garnish

**Variation** This recipe works well with other shellfish, as well as chicken wings and drumsticks. It makes a tangy addition to a barbecue.

**1** Devein the prawns and remove the feelers and legs. Rinse well, pat dry and, using a sharp knife, make an incision along the curve of the tail.

**2** Put the tamarind pulp in a bowl and add 250ml/8fl oz/1 cup warm water. Soak the pulp until soft, squeezing it with your fingers to help soften it. Strain the liquid and discard any fibre.

**3** In a bowl, mix together the tamarind juice, *kecap manis*, sugar and black pepper. Pour it over the prawns, rubbing it over the shells and into the incision in the tails. Cover and leave to marinate for 1 hour.

**4** Prepare the charcoal, or heat the conventional grill (broiler) to a high heat, and place the prawns on the rack. Grill (broil) the prawns for about 3 minutes on each side until cooked through, brushing them with the marinade as they cook. Serve immediately, garnished with coriander and chillies.

**Per Portion** Energy 74Kcal/309kJ; Protein 11.4g; Carbohydrate 4.9g, of which sugars 4.8g; Fat 1.1g, of which saturates 0.3g; Cholesterol 39mg; Calcium 97mg; Fibre 0.6g; Sodium 1301mg.

# Oyster omelette

Often devoured as a late-night treat, oyster omelette, *or luah*, is a favourite hawker stall snack in Singapore. Almost decadent in its rich use of oysters, this is a tasty and satisfying dish, inspired by the Chinese.

**1** Heat the oil in a heavy frying pan. Stir in the garlic and chilli until they become fragrant. Add the large oysters and cook for 1 minute, then stir in the soy sauce and Chinese wine. Season with salt and black pepper.

**2** Pour in the beaten egg mixture and, using a wooden spatula, pull it back from the edge of the pan until it begins to set.

**3** Reduce the heat. Scatter the small oysters over the top of the egg and drizzle with chilli oil. Cover the pan and leave to steam for 5–10 minutes until firm. Sprinkle the omelette with chopped coriander, cut it into wedges and serve it from the pan.

**Serves two**

30ml/2 tbsp vegetable oil

2 garlic cloves, finely chopped

1 red chilli, finely chopped

8 large fresh oysters, shelled and rinsed

15ml/1 tbsp light soy sauce

15ml/1 tbsp Chinese wine

4 eggs, lightly beaten with 30ml/2 tbsp milk

8 small fresh oysters, shelled and rinsed

chilli oil

salt and ground black pepper

fresh coriander (cilantro) leaves, finely chopped, to garnish

**Per Portion** Energy 370Kcal/1543kJ; Protein 32.2g; Carbohydrate 6.1g, of which sugars 1.3g; Fat 24.6g, of which saturates 4.9g; Cholesterol 481mg; Calcium 322mg; Fibre 0g; Sodium 1573mg.

**Serves four**

12 chicken wings

fresh coriander (cilantro) leaves, roughly chopped, and 2–3 green chillies, seeded and quartered lengthways, to garnish

For the spice paste

4 shallots, chopped

4 garlic cloves, chopped

25g/1oz fresh root ginger, chopped

8 red chillies, seeded and chopped

1 lemon grass stalk, trimmed and chopped

30ml/2 tbsp sesame or groundnut (peanut) oil

15ml/1 tbsp tomato purée (paste)

10ml/2 tsp sugar

juice of 2 limes

salt and ground black pepper

# Chargrilled spicy chicken wings

Whole chickens or just the wings and drumsticks, marinated in spicy or tangy pastes and then grilled over charcoal or fried, are a common sight in the food stalls of Malaysia and Singapore. Spicy wings and drumsticks are very popular as a quick snack, which can even be enjoyed on the move. They are often served on their own with a few sprigs of coriander and slices of chilli to munch on, or they form part of the wide selection of dishes on display at the *tze char* stalls, where people fill their bowls with whatever they want.

**1** First make the spice paste. Using a mortar and pestle or food processor, grind the shallots, garlic, ginger, chillies and lemon grass to a paste. Bind with the oil and stir in the tomato purée, sugar and lime juice. Season with salt and pepper. Rub the spice paste into the chicken wings and leave to marinate for 2 hours.

**2** Prepare the charcoal grill. Lift the wings out of the marinade and place them on the rack. Cook them for about 5 minutes each side until cooked through, brushing with marinade while they cook. Serve immediately, garnished with coriander and chillies.

**Per Portion** Energy 350Kcal/1455kJ; Protein 30.7g; Carbohydrate 2.6g, of which sugars 2.6g; Fat 24.1g, of which saturates 5.9g; Cholesterol 134mg; Calcium 11mg; Fibre 0.1g; Sodium 99mg.

# Spicy lentil and meat patties

Otherwise known as shami kebabs, these lentil and lamb patties are popular on the Malay and Muslim stalls, which are often grouped together. Although of Indian origin, the shami kebabs of Malaysia and Singapore have been adapted to suit the local tastes, often served with rice and a sambal, or even between chunks of bread with tomato ketchup, like a burger.

**Serves four**

150g/5oz/generous ½ cup red, brown, yellow or green lentils, rinsed

30ml/2 tbsp vegetable oil

2 onions, finely chopped

2 garlic cloves, finely chopped

1 green chilli, seeded and finely chopped

25g/1oz fresh root ginger, finely chopped

250g/9oz lean minced (ground) lamb

10ml/2 tsp Indian curry powder

5ml/1 tsp turmeric powder

4 eggs

vegetable oil, for shallow frying

salt and ground black pepper

fresh coriander (cilantro) leaves, roughly chopped, to garnish

1 lemon, quartered, to serve

**Variation** The patties are delicious served in a baguette, halved lengthways, layered with lettuce leaves, coriander, mint, yogurt and a hot chutney or a chilli sauce.

**1** Put the lentils in a pan and cover with plenty of water. Bring to a gentle boil and cook until they have softened but still have a bite to them – this can take 20–40 minutes depending on the type of lentil. Drain well.

**2** Heat the oil in a heavy pan and stir in the onions, garlic, chilli and ginger. Fry until they begin to colour, then add the lentils and minced lamb. Cook for a few minutes, then add the curry powder and turmeric. Season with salt and pepper and cook the mixture over a high heat until the moisture has evaporated. The mixture needs to be dry for the patties.

**3** Leave the meat mixture aside until it is cool enough to handle. Beat one of the eggs in a bowl and mix it into the meat. Using your fingers, take small portions of the mixture and roll them into balls about the size of a plum or apricot. Press each ball in the palm of your hand to form thick, flat patties – if the mixture is sticky, wet your palms with a little water.

**4** Beat the remaining eggs in a bowl. Heat enough oil in a heavy pan for shallow frying. Dip each patty in the beaten egg and place them all into the oil. Fry for about 3–4 minutes each side until golden. Garnish with fresh coriander and serve with lemon wedges to squeeze over.

**Per Portion** Energy 488Kcal/2033kJ; Protein 28g; Carbohydrate 25.7g, of which sugars 3.7g; Fat 31.2g, of which saturates 7.4g; Cholesterol 238mg; Calcium 87mg; Fibre 3.1g; Sodium 140mg.

# Popiah

This Nonya creation is a great do-it-yourself dish. Its closest relative is perhaps the Vietnamese rice paper roll, where the wraps and ingredients are fresh and self-assembled at the dinner table.

**1** Heat the oil in a wok or heavy pan. Fry the tofu until golden brown. Remove from the oil and pat dry on kitchen paper.

**2** Fry the garlic and bacon in the oil until they begin to colour. Stir in the fermented soya beans and fresh prawns. Add the *jicama*, bamboo shoots, soy sauce and sugar. Fry over a high heat to reduce the water released from the *jicama*. Toss in the fried tofu and cook the mixture gently until almost dry. Transfer to a serving dish.

**3** Assemble the remaining ingredients in separate bowls and place them on the table. Place the wraps on a serving plate.

**4** To serve, let everyone help themselves to a wrap. Smear the wrap with the chilli and garlic pastes, followed by the *kecap manis*, then place a lettuce leaf on top followed by a layer of cucumber and beansprouts, and a spoonful of the cooked filling. Add Chinese sausage, prawns and crab meat. Place a few strips of omelette on top with a sprinkling of coriander, then fold the edge of the wrap over the filling, tuck in the ends and roll it into a tight package.

**Fantastic finger food** Served in the home, this dish is often a festive affair, as everyone helps themselves from a selection of fillings and garnishes, which they wrap up in fresh *popiah* wraps, rather like a Mexican tortilla. On the hawker stalls, where *popiah* are served as a quick snack, they are often sealed and deep-fried, more akin to a Chinese spring roll. Fresh *popiah* wraps are available in Asian stores, but as a substitute you could use Mexican tortillas.

**Serves four to six**

45ml/3 tbsp vegetable oil

225g/8oz firm tofu, rinsed, drained and diced

4 garlic cloves, finely chopped

4 rashers (strips) streaky (fatty) bacon, finely sliced

45ml/3 tbsp fermented soya beans (*tau cheo*), mashed to a paste

450g/1lb fresh prawns (shrimp), peeled and deveined

225g/8oz *jicama* (sweet turnip), peeled and shredded

450g/1lb bamboo shoots, rinsed and grated

15ml/1 tbsp dark soy sauce

10ml/2 tsp sugar

4–6 red chillies, seeded and pounded to a paste

6–8 garlic cloves, pounded to a paste

*kecap manis*

12 cos or romaine lettuce leaves, washed and patted dry

1 small cucumber, peeled, seeded and finely shredded

225g/8oz beansprouts, washed and drained

2 Chinese sausages, fried and sliced

225g/8oz cooked prawns (shrimp), peeled

225g/8oz cooked crab meat

3 eggs, beaten and fried to form a plain omelette, sliced into thin ribbons

fresh coriander (cilantro) leaves, roughly chopped

12 *popiah* wraps or Mexican corn tortillas

**Per Portion** Energy 457Kcal/1916kJ; Protein 32.3g; Carbohydrate 39.2g, of which sugars 5.8g; Fat 20.1g, of which saturates 4.9g; Cholesterol 213mg; Calcium 396mg; Fibre 4.5g; Sodium 989mg.

**Serves four**

500g/1¼lb pork fillet, cut into bitesize strips, or cubes

salt and ground black pepper

bamboo or wooden skewers

**For the marinade**

4 shallots, chopped

4 garlic cloves, chopped

5ml/1 tsp ground coriander

5ml/1 tsp ground cumin

2.5ml/½ tsp ground turmeric

30ml/2 tbsp dark soy sauce

30ml/2 tbsp sesame or groundnut (peanut) oil

fresh coriander (cilantro) leaves, roughly chopped, to garnish

**For the sauce**

4 shallots, chopped

2 garlic cloves, chopped

4 dried red chillies, soaked in warm water until soft, seeded and chopped

1 lemon grass stalk, trimmed and chopped

25g/1oz fresh root ginger, chopped

30ml/2 tbsp sesame or groundnut (peanut) oil

200ml/7fl oz/scant 1 cup coconut milk

10ml/2 tsp tamarind paste

10ml/2 tsp palm sugar

1 fresh pineapple, peeled, cored and cut into slices

# Pork satay with piquant pineapple sauce

A popular dish at Malay food stalls, satay is the Malay and Indonesian answer to Middle Eastern kebabs. Marinated strips of beef (not for Hindus), chicken, goat, lamb, duck, seafood or pork (not for Muslims) are threaded on to skewers, grilled over charcoal and traditionally served with a piquant peanut sauce. The Indonesians often mix minced lamb or pork with a spice paste and wrap it around skewers, whereas pork satay with pineapple sauce is a Nonya speciality.

**1** First make the marinade. Using a mortar and pestle or food processor, grind the shallots and garlic to form a paste. Stir in the spices and soy sauce and bind with the oil. Rub the marinade into the meat. Cover and set aside for 2 hours at room temperature, or in the refrigerator if leaving for longer than 2 hours.

**2** Meanwhile, prepare the sauce. Using a mortar and pestle or food processor, pound the shallots, garlic, chillies, lemon grass and ginger to form a paste.

**3** Heat the oil in a heavy pan and stir in the paste. Cook for 2–3 minutes until fragrant and beginning to colour, then stir in the coconut milk, tamarind paste and sugar. Bring the mixture to the boil, then reduce the heat and simmer for 5 minutes. Season to taste and leave to cool.

**4** Using a mortar and pestle or a food processor, crush three pineapple slices and beat them into the sauce. Soak the skewers in cold water.

**5** Prepare the charcoal grill and thread the marinated meat on to the skewers. Arrange the skewers over the hot charcoal and place the remaining slices of pineapple beside them. Char the pineapple slices and chop them into chunks. Grill the meat until just cooked, about 2–3 minutes each side, and serve immediately with the pineapple chunks and the sauce.

**Per Portion** Energy 294Kcal/1233kJ; Protein 27.5g; Carbohydrate 16.4g, of which sugars 16g; Fat 13.6g, of which saturates 3g; Cholesterol 79mg; Calcium 47mg; Fibre 1.4g; Sodium 145mg.

# Rice & noodles

# Rice & noodles

Throughout South-east Asia, rice is a staple crop, and in Malaysia and Singapore it is essential in almost every Chinese, Malay, Peranakan and Indian meal. The various types of rice – long and short grain, white, black and glutinous – are used in both sweet and savoury dishes. Noodles – steamed, cooked in broth, or boiled and then stir-fried, are a popular alternative to rice. They are often made with rice flour, demonstrating yet further the versatility of this grain, but wheat noodles also feature in many dishes.

## Rice

All the rice for the region is grown on the Malaysian peninsula. The northern state of Kedah, near the Thai border, produces the bulk of the country's rice. A variety of long, short and sticky rice grains are grown in the region, but the long grain jasmine rice from neighbouring Thailand is particularly prized for its fragrant aroma and flavour. Generally, long and short grain rice is steamed by the absorption method in a heavy pan, or a more modern purpose-built rice cooker, and served in a bowl as the perfect accompaniment to almost every fried, grilled or curried

dish, as well as some soups. Long and short grain rices are also stir-fried in Chinese-style dishes and boiled in plain rice porridge, which is a favourite among the Chinese, especially the Teochews, who serve it with a selection of pickles, strips of omelette and braised or stewed dishes. With a preference for strong tastes, the Malays often flavour their version of rice porridge, *bubur*, with ginger, cinnamon, star anise and coconut and serve it with chillies or a chilli *sambal*.

The Indian communities happily cook with the local rice but, when it comes to special family celebrations

and religious festivals, they prefer to use their own basmati rice, which they cook in ghee to make aromatic pilaffs and *biryani*.

Glutinous rice, which comes in short and long grain varieties, is either black or white. The Chinese, the Peranakans and the small percentage of Thai and Vietnamese residents enjoy glutinous rice moulded into sweet and savoury snacks. They also simmer it with sugar to make their favourite soupy puddings and sweet porridge.

Although the Malays use black glutinous rice to make a sweet porridge, *bubur hitam*, which is served with coconut milk, they generally reserve the glutinous grains for *lemang*. Traditionally, *lemang* is cooked in the hollows of bamboo tubes, lined with banana leaves, which impart a unique flavour and aroma to the rice. In some villages and roadside stalls, you see lines of bamboo poles smoking over charcoal fires for hours, until the rice is cooked and the bamboo is split open to extract a perfectly shaped log of rice, which is sliced into portions and eaten as a snack, or served with a local curry, or the traditional *rendang*, beef cooked in coconut milk.

**Left** *A rice farmer checking his crop in the paddy field.*

Another Malay dish made with moulded rice is *ketupat* – short grain rice, simmered in coconut palm frond baskets for 4–5 hours, to produce small cubes of pressed rice which are traditionally eaten with satay or curries.

For the Malays, the day usually starts with *nasi lemak*, a fragrant coconut rice, which they love topped with fried dried anchovies, *ikan bilis goreng*, and a spicy *sambal*. At the hawker stalls and coffee shops, *nasi lemak* is often served wrapped in a banana leaf, shaped into a cone, topped with a few slices of cucumber, or it is offered with fried chicken, *rendang*, fried egg or deep-fried fish. The big rice stalls offer a selection of rice dishes, as well as a choice of dishes to accompany the rice. In addition to *nasi lemak*, there is *nasi kuning*, yellow rice, plain steamed rice and stir-fried rice. In contrast to these busy, colourful rice stalls, there is also the economy stall that only serves bowls of plain white rice to which a small choice of dishes may be added.

In Singapore, some of the night stalls serve *nasi bubur*, which is the traditional Malay rice porridge, only here it is accompanied by some exciting

**Left** *Short grain rice is used for* ketupat *– compressed rice cakes.*

dishes, such as grilled or fried stingray wings, fried spicy quail and pickled garlic. Some rice stalls sell the blue-tinted rice dish, *nasi kerabu*, a speciality from Kelantan, where the dye is extracted from soaked pea-flower petals.

## Noodles

Chinese immigrants, who introduced rice to large areas of South-east Asia, also brought noodles, which have become hugely popular in Malaysia and Singapore. As most immigrants came from southern China, the noodles are predominantly made from rice flour, wheat and egg or mung beans. Plain wheat noodles, which come from northern China, are mainly found in restaurants specializing in food from that region.

Apart from mung bean thread noodles, which are only sold dried, tied in bundles, the noodles can be bought fresh or dried. Noodle (*mee*) stalls are bathed in the sweet, enticing aroma of stir-fried noodles with ginger and garlic, amid the steam rising from cauldrons of simmering noodle soup. Egg noodles, made with egg and wheat flour, form the basis of many dry stir-fried dishes, which usually include a splash of soy sauce and a sweet Chinese sauce, or even ketchup. Thick, robust Hokkein egg noodles are popular at the Chinese and Malay hawker stalls, where they are cooked in *hokkein mee* with squid, tiny prawns (shrimp), pork and vegetables, and *mee goreng*, a spicy Malay dish with

**Right** *Noodles are popular in soups and form the basis of many stir-fried dishes.*

potato and cabbage, which Indian stalls sell too. Broad rice flour noodles (*mee fen*) form the cornerstone of one of the most popular hawker dishes, *char kway teow*, where they are cooked with squid, prawns and Chinese sausage in a sweet sauce; *laksa* rice noodles (*laksa mee*) are white and fairly thick, ideal for the soupy laksa dishes; and the Malay rice vermicelli, *beehoon*, are wiry and brittle, requiring a soaking in water to soften them before use. Simply stir-fried with vegetables and fresh or dried shrimp, *beehoon* are cooked daily for lunch in Malay and Chinese households. *Beehoon* are also cooked in *mee siam*, a tangy Thai-influenced noodle dish.

Dried mung bean thread noodles, *tung fen*, are delicate, thin and wiry and require soaking before stir-frying. When cooked, they turn transparent, hence their other names, Cellophane or glass noodles. In Singapore and Kuala Lumpur there is a growing craze for instant noodles, used for Western-style snacks, such as fried noodles with a fried egg on top and a dollop of tomato ketchup.

**Serves four**

30ml/2 tbsp vegetable or sesame oil

3 shallots, finely chopped

2 garlic cloves, finely chopped

450g/1lb/generous 2 cups long grain rice, thoroughly washed and drained

400ml/14fl oz/1$^2$/$_3$ cups coconut milk

10ml/2 tsp ground turmeric

4 fresh curry leaves

2.5ml/$^1$/$_2$ tsp salt

ground black pepper

2 red chillies, seeded and finely sliced, to garnish

# Malay yellow rice

Coloured yellow by vibrant turmeric powder, *nasi kuning* is a delicately flavoured rice often served at Malay festivals. It is also one of the popular dishes at the Malay *nasi campur* and Indonesian *nasi padang* stalls, where it is served with a variety of meat and vegetable dishes. Regular long grain, such as jasmine rice, short grain or sticky rice can be used for this dish, which is cooked in the same way as plain steamed rice, using the absorption method.

**1** Heat the oil in a heavy pan and stir in the shallots and garlic. Just as they begin to colour, stir in the rice until it is coated in the oil.

**2** Add the coconut milk, 450ml/$^3$/$_4$ pint/scant 2 cups water, turmeric, curry leaves, salt and pepper. Bring to the boil, then turn down the heat and cover. Cook gently for 15–20 minutes, until all the liquid has been absorbed.

**3** Turn off the heat and leave the rice to steam in the pan for 10 minutes. Fluff up the rice with a fork and serve garnished with red chillies.

**Per Portion** Energy 481Kcal/2011kJ; Protein 8.8g; Carbohydrate 95.9g, of which sugars 5.8g; Fat 6.4g, of which saturates 0.9g; Cholesterol 0mg; Calcium 54mg; Fibre 0.2g; Sodium 356mg.

# Fragrant coconut rice

*Nasi lemak*, fragrant coconut rice, is particularly favoured by the Malay and Peranakan. In rice stalls and coffee shops, it is often served wrapped in banana leaves for breakfast or with a variety of dishes on one plate. A typical plate might include a curry, fried chicken or fish, *rendang*, hard-boiled quail's eggs, strips of cucumber, roasted peanuts and a condiment, such as *acar awak*, the popular vegetable pickle. The Malays are particularly fond of their *nasi lemak* with *sambal ikan bilis*, a sauce made with dried anchovies, chillies and spices, whereas the Peranakans tend to top theirs with *sambal belacan*, the ubiquitous chilli and shrimp paste.

**1** Heat the coconut milk in a heavy pan and stir in the rice with a little salt. Add the pandanus leaf and bring the liquid to the boil. Reduce the heat and simmer until the liquid has been absorbed.

**2** Turn off the heat and cover the pan with a clean dish towel and the lid. Leave the rice to steam for a further 15–20 minutes, then fluff it up with a fork and serve.

### Serves four

1 litre/1¾ pints/4 cups coconut milk

450g/1lb/2¼ cups short grain rice, thoroughly washed and drained

1 pandanus (screwpine) leaf, tied in a loose knot

salt

**Per Portion** Energy 459Kcal/1927kJ; Protein 9.1g; Carbohydrate 102g, of which sugars 12.3g; Fat 1.3g, of which saturates 0.5g; Cholesterol 0mg; Calcium 94mg; Fibre 0g; Sodium 275mg.

# Aromatic Indian pilaff with peas

This fragrant, versatile rice dish is often served as part of an elaborate meal at Indian festivals and celebratory feasts, which include several meat and vegetable curries, a yogurt dish, and chutneys. On occasion, ground turmeric or grated carrot is added for an extra splash of colour. Sprinkle the pilaff with chopped fresh mint and coriander (cilantro), if you like, or with roasted chilli and coconut.

**1** Rinse the rice and put it in a bowl. Cover with plenty of water and leave to soak for 30 minutes. Drain thoroughly.

**2** Heat the ghee, or oil and butter, in a heavy pan. Stir in the cinnamon stick, cardamom and cloves. Add the onion, ginger and sugar, and fry until golden. Add the peas, followed by the rice, and stir for 1 minute to coat the rice in ghee.

**3** Pour in 600ml/1 pint/2½ cups water with the salt, stir once and bring the liquid to the boil. Reduce the heat and allow to simmer for 15–20 minutes, until all the liquid has been absorbed.

**Serves four**

350g/12oz/1¾ cups basmati rice

45ml/3 tbsp ghee or 30ml/2 tbsp vegetable oil and a little butter

1 cinnamon stick

6–8 cardamom pods, crushed

4 cloves

1 onion, halved lengthways and sliced

25g/1oz fresh root ginger, peeled and grated

5ml/1 tsp sugar

130g/4½oz fresh peas, shelled

5ml/1 tsp salt

**Variation** This Indian pilaff also works with diced carrot or beetroot (beet), or chickpeas. Instead of turmeric, you can add a little tomato paste to give the rice a red tinge.

**4** Turn off the heat, cover the pan with a clean dishtowel and the lid, and leave the rice to steam for a further 10 minutes. Spoon the rice on to a serving dish.

**Per Portion** Energy 451Kcal/1880kJ; Protein 8.9g; Carbohydrate 75.7g, of which sugars 2.6g; Fat 12.2g, of which saturates 5.4g; Cholesterol 0mg; Calcium 28mg; Fibre 1.8g; Sodium 328mg.

**Serves four**

225g/8oz/generous 1 cup short grain rice, thoroughly washed and drained

2.5ml/½ tsp salt

dipping sauce, to serve

4 x 20cm/8in by 30cm/12in sheets of foil

# Compressed rice cakes

In Malaysia, these compressed rice cakes, *ketupat*, are cooked in little woven packages made from strips of palm fronds and served with satay. The packages containing uncooked rice are tied in bundles and lowered into a deep pan of boiling water, where they are left to simmer over a very low heat for about 3 hours. To make *ketupat* in a Western home, it's easier to pre-cook the rice and then steam it in banana leaves, which are available in Asian markets, or in foil packages.

**1** In a heavy pan, bring 600ml/1 pint/2½ cups water to the boil. Stir in the rice and salt, reduce the heat and allow to simmer for about 20 minutes, until all the water has been absorbed.

**2** Meanwhile prepare a steamer – a bamboo basket set into a wok, or a conventional steamer. Spoon one-quarter of the rice about 2.5cm/1in in from the shorter edge of each foil sheet, then roll up loosely to leave room for the rice to expand. Twist the ends to seal, so they resemble Christmas crackers. Place the parcels in the steamer and cook gently for 40 minutes.

**3** Leave the parcels to cool, twisting them more tightly if necessary, before unwrapping. Slice the compressed rice into bitesize rounds and serve with a Malay curry dish, satay or simply with soy sauce, or a *sambal*, for dipping.

**Per Portion** Energy 202Kcal/845kJ; Protein 4.2g; Carbohydrate 44.9g, of which sugars 0g; Fat 0.3g, of which saturates 0g; Cholesterol 0mg; Calcium 11mg; Fibre 0g; Sodium 164mg.

# Bubur

Originating from China, this thick rice porridge has become popular all over South-east Asia. Designed to be nourishing and bland, the joy is derived from the ingredients, or dishes, added to it.

**1** Bring 1.2 litres/2 pints/5 cups water to the boil in a heavy pan. Stir in the spices, the salt and the rice.

**2** Reduce the heat, cover the pan, and simmer gently for 1 hour, or longer if you prefer a thicker, smoother consistency. Serve steaming hot.

**Serves four to six**

25g/1oz fresh root ginger, peeled and sliced

1 cinnamon stick

2 star anise

2.5ml/$\frac{1}{2}$ tsp salt

115g/4oz/$\frac{1}{2}$ cup short grain rice, thoroughly washed and drained

**Varieties of bubur** The Teochew version of *bubur* is called *muay*. With its addition of pickles, strips of omelette and braised dishes, it is popular for supper in Singapore. *Bubur*, the Malay name for rice porridge, is enjoyed for breakfast with fried or grilled fish, chicken and beef, as well as pickles. Often flavoured with ginger, cinnamon and star anise, *bubur* is usually cooked until it is thick but the grains are still visible, whereas some of the Chinese versions are cooked for longer so that the rice breaks down completely. The consistency varies from family to family as some like it soupy and eat it with a spoon.

**Per Portion** Energy 69Kcal/288kJ; Protein 1.4g; Carbohydrate 15.3g, of which sugars 0g; Fat 0.1g, of which saturates 0g; Cholesterol 0mg; Calcium 4mg; Fibre 0g; Sodium 164mg.

# Indian lentils with ginger and coconut milk

Though not a rice or noodle dish, dhal (meaning either lentils or the cooked dish) is so popular – either eaten simply with rice or Indian bread, or as part of a more elaborate meal – that it could not be left out. For the largely vegetarian South Indian immigrants who introduced it, dhal is an important source of protein.

**1** Heat the ghee, or oil and butter, in a heavy pan. Stir in the onion, garlic, chillies and ginger and fry until fragrant and beginning to colour. Add the sugar, cumin seeds, turmeric and garam masala, taking care not to burn the spices. Stir in the lentils and coat in the spices and ghee. Pour in 600ml/1 pint/2½ cups water, mix thoroughly, and bring to the boil. Reduce the heat and allow to simmer gently for 35–40 minutes until the mixture is thick.

**2** Stir in the coconut milk and continue to simmer for a further 30 minutes until thick and mushy – if at any time the dhal seems too dry, add more water or coconut milk. Season to taste with salt.

**3** In a small pan, heat the mustard seeds. As soon as they begin to pop, add the curry leaves and chillies. When the chillies begin to darken, stir in the ghee until it melts. Spoon the mixture over the dhal, or fold it in until well mixed. Serve the dhal with yogurt or with a curry, rice and chutney.

### Serves four

30ml/2 tbsp ghee, or 15ml/1 tbsp vegetable oil and 15g/½oz/1 tbsp butter

1 onion, chopped

4 garlic cloves, chopped

2 red chillies, seeded and chopped

50g/2oz fresh root ginger, peeled and chopped

10ml/2 tsp sugar

7.5ml/1½ tsp cumin seeds

5ml/1 tsp ground turmeric

15ml/1 tbsp garam masala

225g/8oz/generous 1 cup brown lentils, washed thoroughly and drained

600ml/1 pint/2½ cups coconut milk

salt

yogurt or curry, rice and chutney, to serve

### For the garnish

10ml/2 tsp mustard seeds

a small handful dried curry leaves

1–2 dried red chillies

15ml/1 tbsp ghee

**Per Portion** Energy 322Kcal/1358kJ; Protein 14g; Carbohydrate 41.3g, of which sugars 10.6g; Fat 12.4g, of which saturates 5.7g; Cholesterol 0mg; Calcium 77mg; Fibre 3g; Sodium 186mg.

**Serves four**

30ml/2 tbsp vegetable oil

1 carrot, cut into matchsticks

225g/8oz fresh prawns (shrimp), peeled

120ml/4fl oz/½ cup chicken stock or water

30ml/2 tbsp light soy sauce

15ml/1 tbsp dark soy sauce

175g/6oz beansprouts

115g/4oz mustard greens or pak choi (bok choy), shredded

225g/8oz dried rice vermicelli, soaked in lukewarm water until pliable, and drained

1–2 fresh red chillies, seeded and finely sliced, and fresh coriander (cilantro) leaves, roughly chopped, to garnish

**For the *rempah***

4 dried red chillies, soaked until soft and seeded

4 garlic cloves, chopped

4 shallots, chopped

25g/1oz fresh root ginger, peeled and chopped

5ml/1 tsp ground turmeric

# Malay beehoon

In Malaysia and Singapore, there are endless stir-fried noodle dishes. Some of these are classic Chinese recipes; others have been influenced by the Chinese but adapted to suit the tastes of the different communities. *Beehoon* is the Malay name for the rice vermicelli which, in this popular snack, are stir-fried with prawns and lots of chilli.

**1** Using a mortar and pestle or food processor, grind the ingredients for the *rempah* to a paste.

**2** Heat the oil in a wok or heavy pan, and stir in the *rempah* until it begins to colour and become fragrant. Toss in the carrots for a minute, followed by the prawns. Pour in the stock or water and soy sauces and cook for 1 minute.

**3** Add the beansprouts and mustard greens, followed by the noodles. Toss well to make sure the vegetables noodles are well coated and heated through. Transfer to a serving plate and garnish with the sliced chillies and coriander.

**Per Portion** Energy 330Kcal/1377kJ; Protein 17.5g; Carbohydrate 49.9g, of which sugars 4.5g; Fat 6.6g, of which saturates 0.8g; Cholesterol 110mg; Calcium 125mg; Fibre 1.9g; Sodium 960mg.

# Chinese clay pot rice with chicken

This Cantonese dish is a great family one-pot meal. It can also be found on Chinese stalls and in some coffee shops. The traditional clay pot ensures that the ingredients remain moist, while allowing the flavours to mingle, but any earthenware pot such as a Spanish or Portuguese one will do. This recipe also works well with prawns or strips of pork fillet.

**Serves four**

500g/1¼lb chicken breast fillets, cut into thin strips

5 dried shiitake mushrooms, soaked in hot water for 30 minutes, until soft

1 Chinese sausage, sliced

750ml/1¼ pints/3 cups chicken stock

225g/8oz/generous 1 cup long grain rice, thoroughly washed and drained

fresh coriander (cilantro) leaves, finely chopped, to garnish

**For the marinade**

30ml/2 tbsp sesame oil

45ml/3 tbsp oyster sauce

30ml/2 tbsp soy sauce

25g/1oz fresh root ginger, finely grated (shredded)

2 spring onions (scallions), trimmed and finely sliced

1 red chilli, seeded and finely sliced

5ml/1 tsp sugar

ground black pepper

**1** In a bowl, mix together the ingredients for the marinade. Toss in the chicken, making sure it is well coated. Set aside.

**2** Make sure the shiitake mushrooms are soft (leave them to soak for longer, if necessary). Squeeze them to get rid of any excess water. Using a sharp knife, remove any hard stems and halve the caps. Add the mushroom caps and the Chinese sausage to the chicken.

**3** Bring the stock to the boil in the clay pot. Stir in the rice and bring it back to the boil. Reduce the heat, cover the pot, and simmer on a low heat for 15–20 minutes, until almost all the liquid has been absorbed.

**4** Spread the marinated mixture over the top of the rice and cover the pot. Leave to steam for about 10–15 minutes, until all the liquid is absorbed and the chicken is cooked. Garnish with coriander and serve.

**Cook's tip** Remember, if you are using a newly bought clay pot, you need to treat it first. Fill it with water and slowly bring it to the boil. Simmer for 5–10 minutes, then leave it to cool. Pour out the water and wipe the pot dry. Now it is ready to use.

**Per Portion** Energy 371Kcal/1560kJ; Protein 36.2g; Carbohydrate 46.8g, of which sugars 1g; Fat 4g, of which saturates 1.2g; Cholesterol 93mg; Calcium 54mg; Fibre 0.7g; Sodium 721mg.

**Serves four**

30ml/2 tbsp vegetable oil

3 garlic cloves, finely chopped

115g/4oz pork fillet, cut into thin strips

115g/4oz fresh fish fillets (such as red snapper, grouper or trout), cut into bitesize pieces

115g/4oz fresh prawns (shrimp), shelled and deveined

2 small squid, with innards and backbone removed, cleaned and sliced (reserve tentacles)

300ml/½ pint/1¼ cups chicken stock

450g/1lb fresh egg noodles

1 carrot, shredded

6 long white Chinese cabbage leaves, shredded

30ml/2 tbsp dark soy sauce

30ml/2 tbsp light soy sauce

ground black pepper

a small bunch of fresh coriander (cilantro), roughly chopped

# Singapore egg noodles

Otherwise known as *Hokkein mee,* this is a very popular stir-fried dish in Singapore, where the majority of the Chinese population is Hokkein. The dish takes its name from the people, as well as from the thick egg noodles, commonly called Hokkein noodles, which are also used in Malay and Indian hawker dishes. Filled with squid, prawns, fish and pork, this is a deliciously satisfying meal in itself.

**1** Heat the oil in a wok and stir in the garlic. When it becomes fragrant, stir in the pork, fish, prawns and squid, tossing them around the pan for 1 minute. Pour in the stock and bubble it up to reduce it.

**2** Add the noodles and toss them around the wok for 1 minute. Stir in the shredded carrot and cabbage, add the soy sauces and cook until most of the liquid has evaporated. Season with pepper, sprinkle with coriander, divide the noodles among four bowls and eat while steaming hot.

**Per Portion** Energy 609Kcal/2571kJ; Protein 35.2g; Carbohydrate 84.4g, of which sugars 5.3g; Fat 16.9g, of which saturates 3.8g; Cholesterol 186mg; Calcium 81mg; Fibre 4.2g; Sodium 867mg.

# Chinese stir-fried noodles

This Chinese dish of stir-fried rice noodles and seafood, *char kway teow*, is one of the most popular at the hawker stalls. Breakfast, lunch, supper, mid-morning, mid-afternoon or late evening, there's always *char kway teow* on the go. Variations include red snapper, clams and pork. *Kway teow* is in fact the name for the broad, fresh rice noodles available in Chinese markets.

**1** Heat a wok and add the oil. Stir in the garlic and chillies and fry until fragrant. Add the Chinese sausage, followed by the prawns and squid, tossing them to mix thoroughly.

**2** Toss in the noodles and mix well. Add the soy sauce and *kecap manis*, and toss in the mustard leaves and beansprouts.

**3** Quickly stir in the eggs for a few seconds until set. Season with black pepper, garnish with coriander and serve immediately.

**Serves three to four**

45ml/3 tbsp vegetable oil

2 garlic cloves, finely chopped

2 red chillies, seeded and finely sliced

1 Chinese sausage, finely sliced

12 fresh prawns (shrimp), peeled

2 small squid, trimmed, cleaned, skinned and sliced

500g/1¼lb fresh rice noodles

30ml/2 tbsp light soy sauce

45ml/3 tbsp *kecap manis*

2–3 mustard green leaves, chopped

a handful of beansprouts

2 eggs, lightly beaten

ground black pepper

fresh coriander (cilantro) leaves, finely chopped, to serve

**Cook's tip** You can replace *kecap manis* with the same quantity of dark soy sauce mixed with a little sugar.

Per Portion Energy 618Kcal/2582kJ; Protein 24.8g; Carbohydrate 100g, of which sugars 1.1g; Fat 12.9g, of which saturates 2.1g; Cholesterol 217mg; Calcium 96mg; Fibre 0.5g; Sodium 717mg.

# Fish & shellfish

# Fish & shellfish

Set apart from the vegetables and fruit, fish and shellfish are located in the wettest part of the markets. While the stallholders slosh about in black or yellow rubber boots, the night's catch is displayed next to the meat section, and is flanked by bunches of bright scarlet-, violet-, amber-, saffron- and pearl-coloured flowers. Nearby the stacks of dried goods, such as rice, dried shrimp and squid, sharks' fins and *popiah* wrappers, supply the rest of the cook's needs.

The variety and quantity of fish and shellfish caught off the coasts of Malaysia and Singapore are stupendous. Added to the bounty from the sea, there is a plentiful supply of freshwater fish caught in the network of river systems that drain the mountainous regions and jungles throughout the Malaysian peninsula, Sabah and Sarawak. And the markets display all of these: sea and freshwater prawns (shrimp), blue swimmer crabs from the sea and mud crabs from the mangrove swamps; squid, mussels, cockles and clams; jellyfish; white pomfret; freshwater carp; mackerel; sea bass; grouper; snapper; and sea cucumber, *trepang*, which the Chinese use in braised dishes.

## Regional cooking methods

The Malays generally prefer their fish fried whole and stuffed with spices, or chopped into chunks or steaks, which they fry or grill and serve with a spicy tamarind sauce or chilli *sambal*. The Chinese stir-fry shellfish, but prefer to cook larger fish, such as snapper, sea bass and grouper, by steaming or braising to preserve the delicate flavours. The Chinese also have a liking for jellyfish, which is often sliced into strips and tossed in a sesame oil and rice vinegar dressing, a dish appreciated more for its texture than taste.

Fish dishes vary from region to region, depending on the local mix of culinary cultures, and no dish exemplifies this as much as the spicy, soupy noodle favourite, *laksa*, which alternates between wolf herring, mackerel, scallops and prawns. Mackerel is the favoured fish for *otak otak*, spicy fish cakes, wrapped in banana leaves and grilled over a charcoal fire. Plump pomfret is prized for Chinese and Nonya dishes, particularly when it is steamed gently with pickled sour plums and salted cabbage. Stingray is a hot seller at the hawker stalls and coffee shops in Singapore, where the wings are grilled and served in a banana leaf with chilli *sambal*. Fish balls, made with the flesh of meaty fish such as mackerel or pomfret, are an essential ingredient in Singaporean dishes. Adopted from the

**Right** *Chargrilled stingray wings are served with a hot chilli* sambal.

Teochew Chinese, the flesh is pounded with salt to form a paste, which is then moulded into balls. Added to soups or used as garnishes for noodles, or served on their own with a dipping sauce, these Singapore fish balls are light and versatile. The heads of any large fish, such as grouper or snapper, are cooked in the Indian-inspired fish head curry, which has become a classic in Singapore and some southern parts of Malaysia.

## Shellfish

Fresh shellfish finds its way into endless soups, soupy noodles, stir-fried noodles and rice, and curries. In the small fishing villages, cockles are collected, cleaned and bagged for distribution to the big cities like Kuala Lumpur, Terengganu and Singapore. About 5000kg/11,000lb of cockles pass through each processing plant every day, destined for popular noodle and rice dishes, such as the hawker favourites, *char kway teow* and Singapore *laksa*. The Malays and Peranakans also serve cooked cockles as a snack with a bowl of chilli-flavoured

vinegar to dip them in. Clams, mussels and oysters are farmed in the coastal waters off the Malaysian peninsula. The Peranakans like to stir-fry clams with curry paste and lemon grass, and the oysters are memorable in a satisfying omelette, *or lua*, which is one of the late-night hawker specialities. Prawns are delicious marinated in tamarind and spices and chargrilled in their shells, and the Chinese tend to steam whole crabs with aromatic herbs and spices. An all-time favourite, though, is Singapore's speciality of stir-fried chilli crab.

In Malaysia and Singapore, prawns, squid and anchovies are dried mainly for Malay and Chinese dishes. Dried squid is generally added to soup stocks and Chinese broths, and dried anchovies are fried with peanuts for a quick snack with chunks of bread, or they are served as an accompaniment to coconut rice, *nasi lemak*, and the Malay rice porridge, *bubur*.

**Right** *Squid is cooked fresh or dried and added to soups.*

Dried shrimp are used throughout Malaysia in a number of stocks, fillings and pastes for texture and flavour. The tiny shrimp pulled out of the Strait of Melaka are left to ferment in salt to make *cincaluk*, fermented shrimps, and *belacan*, the pungent fermented shrimp paste. *Cincaluk* is generally added to *sambals* for body and flavour, or it is served as a snack with chopped shallots, chillies and lime juice. *Belacan*, on the other hand, forms an intrinsic part of many Malay and Peranakan dishes, as it is pounded with chillies to make *sambal belacan*, the ever-popular Malay condiment. It is also ground into many of the spice pastes and it is added to soups, curries, and marinades for its unique flavouring. The blocks of quality shrimp paste should be pungent, smelling of fish and the sea, not stomach-churning like the low-grade *belacan*, which stinks of rotten fish.

**Serves two**

30ml/2 tbsp ghee or vegetable oil

10ml/2 tsp brown mustard seeds

5ml/1 tsp fenugreek seeds

5ml/1 tsp cumin seeds

a handful of curry leaves

15ml/1 tbsp palm sugar

30ml/2 tbsp tamarind pulp, soaked in 150ml/$^1/_4$ pint/$^2/_3$ cup water and strained for juice

600ml/1 pint/$2^1/_2$ cups coconut milk

1 large fresh fish head, such as red snapper (about 900g/2lb), cleaned

5 okra, halved diagonally

2 large tomatoes, skinned, seeded and quartered

salt and ground black pepper

steamed rice and pickles, to serve

**For the spice paste**

8 shallots, chopped

6 garlic cloves, chopped

4 red chillies, seeded and chopped

50g/2oz fresh root ginger, peeled and chopped

25g/1oz fresh turmeric, chopped

1 lemon grass stalk, trimmed and chopped

30ml/2 tbsp fish curry powder

# Fish head curry

The origins of this Singapore street dish have become a little blurred with time. Some people say it came with the immigrants from Kerala in south India; others claim an Indian chef created it in Singapore in the 1950s or 60s. Whatever its origins, *ka li yu tou* is in demand at Indian and Malay food stalls, where there are numerous versions. The best fish head curry, prized for the succulent cheeks, is said to be found at a few select coffee shops in Singapore.

**1** To make the spice paste, grind all the ingredients together using a mortar and pestle or food processor.

**2** Heat the ghee or oil in a wok or heavy pan. Stir in the mustard seeds, fenugreek and cumin seeds along with the curry leaves. Fry until the mustard seeds begin to pop and then stir in the spice paste. Fry until fragrant, then stir in the sugar, followed by the tamarind juice and coconut milk.

**3** Bring to the boil, reduce the heat and add the fish head. Simmer gently for 10 minutes, then add the okra and tomatoes. Simmer for another 10 minutes or until the fish head is cooked. Season the sauce and serve with steamed rice and pickles.

**Per Portion** Energy 417Kcal/1760kJ; Protein 42.2g; Carbohydrate 30.4g, of which sugars 29.1g; Fat 15.2g, of which saturates 2.7g; Cholesterol 74mg; Calcium 231mg; Fibre 2.7g; Sodium 497mg.

# Grilled stingray wings with chilli *sambal*

Chargrilled stingray is a very popular street snack in Singapore. The grill stalls selling grilled chicken wings and satay often serve grilled stingray wings on a banana leaf with a generous dollop of chilli *sambal*. The cooked fish is eaten with fingers, or chopsticks, by tearing off pieces and dipping them in the *sambal*. If you can't find stingray wings, you could substitute a flat fish, such as plaice. Banana leaves are available in Chinese and Asian markets.

**1** First make the chilli *sambal*. Using a mortar and pestle or food processor, grind the chillies with the garlic to form a paste. Beat in the shrimp paste, tomato purée and sugar. Add the lime juice and bind with the oil.

**2** Prepare a charcoal grill. Rub each stingray wing with a little chilli *sambal* and place them on the rack. Cook for 3–4 minutes on each side, until tender. Sprinkle with salt and serve on banana leaves with the remaining chilli *sambal* and the limes.

**Serves four**

4 medium-sized stingray wings, about 200g/7oz, rinsed and patted dry

salt

4 banana leaves, about 30cm/12in square

2 fresh limes, halved

For the chilli *sambal*

6–8 red chillies, seeded and chopped

4 garlic cloves, chopped

5ml/1 tsp shrimp paste

15ml/1 tbsp tomato purée (paste)

15ml/1 tbsp palm sugar

juice of 2 limes

30ml/2 tbsp vegetable or groundnut (peanut) oil

**Per Portion** Energy 195Kcal/823kJ; Protein 30.4g; Carbohydrate 4.5g, of which sugars 4.5g; Fat 6.3g, of which saturates 0.7g; Cholesterol 0mg; Calcium 83mg; Fibre 0.1g; Sodium 249mg.

# Steamed fish Nonya-style

In Malay and Indian cooking, whole fish is often grilled or fried with spices, whereas the Chinese and the Peranakans prefer to steam it. Plump pomfret ranks as one of the favourites to steam whole, often with subtle flavourings so as not to spoil the fresh taste of the fish. This Nonya dish is particularly popular in Penang, Melaka and Singapore, where the Peranakans serve it with a chilli *sambal*.

**1** Put the spring onions and ginger in a bowl. Trim the shiitake mushrooms, discarding the hard stems, and cut them into thin strips. Add them to the spring onions and ginger and mix well.

**2** Fill a wok one-third of the way up with water. Place a metal steaming rack into the wok, cover with the lid and put the wok over the heat. Score the fish diagonally three or four times and season with salt and pepper. Place it on a heatproof plate and scatter the spring onion, ginger and shiitakes over the top. Place the plate on the rack, cover with the lid and steam the fish for 15–20 minutes, until cooked.

**3** When the fish is cooked, heat the oil in a small pan. Stir in the soy sauce and pour it over the fish. Garnish the dish with the chillies and coriander leaves and serve with steamed rice and chilli *sambal*.

**Serves four**

3 spring onions (scallions), trimmed into 2.5cm/1in pieces and cut into strips

25g/1oz fresh root ginger, peeled and cut into 2.5cm/1in strips

4 dried shiitake mushrooms, soaked in hot water until soft and squeezed dry

1 whole fresh fish, such as pomfret or sea bass, weighing about 900g/2lb, gutted and cleaned

30ml/2 tbsp vegetable or sesame oil

30ml/2 tbsp light soy sauce

salt and ground black pepper

1 red chilli, seeded and cut into thin strips and fresh coriander (cilantro) leaves, to garnish

steamed rice and chilli *sambal*, to serve

**Per Portion** Energy 278Kcal/1165kJ; Protein 43.7g; Carbohydrate 0.5g, of which sugars 0.5g; Fat 11.2g, of which saturates 1.6g; Cholesterol 180mg; Calcium 296mg; Fibre 0.1g; Sodium 423mg.

**Serves four**

30ml/2 tbsp vegetable oil

7.5ml/1$\frac{1}{2}$ tsp tamarind paste

8 thick fish cutlets, about 90g/3$\frac{1}{2}$oz, such as grouper, red snapper, trout or mackerel

800ml/1$\frac{1}{2}$ pints coconut milk

salt

fresh coriander (cilantro) leaves, roughly chopped, to garnish

rice or crusty bread, to serve

**For the curry paste**

4 shallots, chopped

4 garlic cloves, chopped

50g/2oz fresh root ginger, peeled and chopped

25g/1oz fresh turmeric, chopped

4–6 dried red chillies, softened in warm water, seeded and chopped

15ml/1 tbsp coriander seeds, roasted

15ml/1 tbsp cumin seeds, roasted

10ml/2 tsp fish curry powder

5ml/1 tsp fennel seeds

2.5ml/$\frac{1}{2}$ tsp black peppercorns

**Cook's tip**  To roast the spices, heat them gently in a dry, heavy pan until they begin to colour and develop a nutty aroma. Take care not to burn them.

# Malay fish curry

The fish curries of Malaysia differ slightly from region to region, but most of them include Indian spices and coconut milk. The Malay food stalls often feature a fish, chicken or beef curry, which is usually served with bread or rice, pickles and extra chillies.

**1** First make the curry paste. Using a mortar and pestle or food processor, grind the shallots, garlic, ginger, turmeric and chillies to a paste and transfer to a bowl. Again, using the mortar and pestle or food processor, grind the roasted coriander and cumin seeds, fish curry powder, fennel seeds and peppercorns to a powder and add to the paste in the bowl. Bind with 15ml/1 tbsp water and thoroughly mix together.

**2** Heat the oil in a wok or heavy pan. Stir in the curry paste and fry until fragrant. Add the tamarind paste and mix well. Add the fish cutlets and cook for 1 minute on each side. Pour in the coconut milk, mix well and bring to the boil. Reduce the heat and simmer for 10–15 minutes until the fish is cooked. Season to taste with salt. Scatter the coriander over the top and serve with plain or yellow rice, or with chunks of crusty bread to mop up the sauce.

**Per Portion** Energy 264Kcal/1109kJ; Protein 36.6g; Carbohydrate 12.7g, of which sugars 12.1g; Fat 7.7g, of which saturates 1.3g; Cholesterol 89mg; Calcium 110mg; Fibre 1g; Sodium 354mg.

**Serves four to six**

175g/6oz fresh tuna or salmon, finely sliced

115g/4oz white fish fillet, finely sliced

25g/1oz fresh root ginger, peeled and finely chopped

2 garlic cloves, crushed

juice of 2 limes

225g/8oz daikon (white radish), cut into julienne strips

2 carrots, cut into julienne strips

1 small cucumber, peeled, seeded and cut into julienne strips

4 spring onions (scallions), trimmed and cut into julienne strips

1 pomelo, segmented and sliced

4 fresh lime leaves, finely sliced

50g/2oz preserved sweet melon, finely sliced

50g/2oz preserved sweet red ginger, finely sliced

ground black pepper

30ml/2 tbsp roasted peanuts, coarsely crushed, to garnish

**For the dressing**

30ml/2 tbsp sesame oil

15ml/1 tbsp light soy sauce

15ml/1 tbsp red vinegar

30ml/2 tbsp sour plum sauce

2 garlic cloves, crushed

10ml/2 tsp sugar

# New Year raw fish salad

To celebrate the lunar New Year, Chinese families in Malaysia and Singapore get together to eat special dishes, such as *yu sheng*, a raw fish salad, which all the diners must help to mix with their chopsticks, while they shout "*lo hei*" ("toss the fish"), as this ensures good luck and abundance. During the New Year period, many of the Chinese restaurants in Singapore offer this dish with the addition of sliced jellyfish among the colourful array of vegetables, some of which have been dyed red and green with food colouring.

**1** In a shallow, non-metallic, dish, toss the fish in the ginger, garlic and lime juice. Season with black pepper and set aside for at least 30 minutes.

**2** Place the daikon, carrots, cucumber, spring onions, pomelo and lime leaves in a large bowl. Add the preserved melon and ginger.

**3** In a small bowl, mix together the ingredients for the dressing. Adjust the sweet and sour balance to taste.

**4** Just before serving, place the marinated fish on top of the vegetables in the bowl. Pour the dressing over the top and sprinkle with the roasted peanuts. Place the bowl in the middle of the table and let everyone toss the salad with their chopsticks.

**Cook's tip** The Chinese add jellyfish to this salad for the texture rather than the taste. If you would like to add a different ingredient for its texture, you could try 50g/2oz cubes of steamed or stir-fried firm tofu.

**Per Portion** Energy 126Kcal/528kJ; Protein 13.2g; Carbohydrate 6.5g, of which sugars 6.4g; Fat 5.4g, of which saturates 1g; Cholesterol 22mg; Calcium 36mg; Fibre 1.3g; Sodium 222mg.

# Spiced fish cakes in banana leaves

The oily flesh of mackerel is generally used for this Nonya dish, *ikan otak-otak*. Mixed with spices, wrapped in banana leaves and baked, steamed or grilled over charcoal, the resulting fish cakes make a tasty addition to a summer dinner, or a picnic snack. They can be eaten hot or cold as fish cakes, or they can be used as little packages of fish paste to spread on toast, fresh bread or cocktail canapés. Banana leaves are available in Chinese and Asian markets, but you could also use prepared vine leaves or foil.

**1** Using a mortar and pestle or food processor, grind the shallots, lemon grass, galangal, candlenuts or macadamia nuts and chillies to a paste. Beat in the shrimp paste and turmeric. Stir in the coconut cream, soy sauce and sugar until blended.

**2** Put the flaked mackerel and lime leaves in a bowl. Pour in the spiced coconut cream and the beaten eggs. Season with salt and pepper. Gently, using a fork or your hand, toss the fish in the coconut cream and eggs, making sure it is well coated.

### Serves four to six

4 shallots, chopped

1 lemon grass stalk, trimmed and chopped

25g/1oz galangal, chopped

4 candlenuts or macadamia nuts, roasted

4 dried red chillies, soaked in warm water until soft, squeezed dry and seeded

5ml/1 tsp shrimp paste

5–10ml/1–2 tsp ground turmeric

250ml/8fl oz/1 cup coconut cream

15ml/1 tbsp dark soy sauce

10ml/2 tsp palm sugar

450g/1lb fresh mackerel, cleaned, skinned and flaked

4–6 kaffir lime leaves, finely shredded

2 eggs, lightly beaten

salt and ground black pepper

12 banana leaves, cut into pieces about 20cm/8in square

cocktail sticks (toothpicks)

2 limes, quartered lengthways, and chilli or peanut *sambal*, to serve

**3** Lay a square of banana leaf on a flat surface. Place 30ml/2 tbsp of the fish mixture just off centre and fold the sides of the leaf over the top, leaving a little room for expansion. Secure the package with a cocktail stick threaded through each end, and repeat with the rest of the mixture.

**4** Preheat the oven to 200°C/400°F/Gas 6 or prepare a charcoal grill. Bake the fish cakes in the oven for 30 minutes or grill them for 15 minutes each side.

**5** Serve the fish cakes in the banana leaves with the lime quarters. Allow each diner to unwrap their leaves and squeeze a little lime juice over the fish cakes, before dipping them into chilli or peanut *sambal*.

**Per Portion** Energy 396Kcal/1642kJ; Protein 19.5g; Carbohydrate 4.5g, of which sugars 4.2g; Fat 33.5g, of which saturates 16.1g; Cholesterol 117mg; Calcium 60mg; Fibre 0.5g; Sodium 382mg.

# Sabahan squid in hot yellow sauce

Simple fishermen's dishes such as this one are cooked the length and breadth of Malaysia's coastline. This recipe from Sabah, the northernmost state in Malaysian Borneo, includes enough chillies to set your tongue on fire. To temper the heat, the dish is often served with the local staple, sago porridge, and finely shredded green mango tossed in lime juice.

**1** First prepare the squid. Hold the body sac in one hand and pull off the head with the other. Sever the tentacles just above the eyes, and discard the rest of the head and innards. Clean the body sac inside and out and remove the skin. Pat the squid dry, cut it into thick slices and put them in a bowl, along with the tentacles. Mix the lime juice with the salt and rub it into the squid. Set aside for 30 minutes.

**2** Meanwhile, using a mortar and pestle or food processor, grind the shallots, garlic, galangal, turmeric and chillies to a coarse paste.

**3** Heat the oil in a wok or heavy pan, and stir in the coarse paste. Cook the paste until fragrant, then stir in the palm sugar, lemon grass and lime leaves. Drain the squid of any juice and toss it around the wok, coating it in the flavourings. Pour in the coconut milk and bring it to the boil. Reduce the heat and simmer for 5–10 minutes, until the squid is tender. Season with salt and pepper and serve with chunks of fresh, crusty bread or steamed rice.

### Serves four

500g/1¼lb fresh squid

juice of 2 limes

5ml/1 tsp salt

4 shallots, chopped

4 garlic cloves, chopped

25g/1oz galangal, chopped

25g/1oz fresh turmeric, chopped

6–8 red chillies, seeded and chopped

30ml/2 tbsp vegetable or groundnut (peanut) oil

7.5ml/1½ tsp palm sugar

2 lemon grass stalks, crushed

4 lime leaves

400ml/14fl oz/1²/₃ cups coconut milk

salt and ground black pepper

crusty bread or steamed rice, to serve

**Per Portion** Energy 185Kcal/780kJ; Protein 19.8g; Carbohydrate 9.4g, of which sugars 7.6g; Fat 8g, of which saturates 1.4g; Cholesterol 281mg; Calcium 50mg; Fibre 0.2g; Sodium 739mg.

# Singapore chilli crab

Perhaps Singapore's signature dish could be chilli crab. An all-time favourite at hawker stalls and coffee shops, steaming woks of crab deep-frying are a common sight. Spicy and delicious, this is a dish where your fingers will get messy. The crabs are placed in the middle of the table with a bowl for the discarded pieces of shell, and small bowls of water for cleaning your fingers. Crack the shells, then dip the meat into the cooking sauce. Mop up the sauce with lots of crusty bread.

**1** Using a mortar and pestle or food processor, grind the ingredients for the spice paste and set aside.

**2** Heat enough oil for deep-frying in a wok or heavy pan. Drop in the crabs and fry until the shells turn bright red. Remove from the oil and drain.

**3** Heat the sesame oil in a wok and stir in the spice paste. Fry until fragrant and stir in the chilli sauce, ketchup, soy sauce and sugar. Toss in the fried crab and coat well in the sauce. Pour in the chicken stock or water and bring to the boil. Reduce the heat and simmer for 5 minutes. Season the sauce to taste.

**4** Pour in the eggs, stirring gently, to let them set in the sauce. Serve immediately, garnished with spring onions and coriander.

### Serves four

vegetable oil, for deep-frying

4 fresh crabs, about 250g/9oz each, cleaned

30ml/2 tbsp sesame oil

30–45ml/2–3 tbsp chilli sauce

45ml/3 tbsp tomato ketchup

15ml/1 tbsp soy sauce

15ml/1 tbsp sugar

250ml/8fl oz/1 cup chicken stock or water

2 eggs, beaten

salt and ground black pepper

2 spring onions (scallions), finely sliced, and fresh coriander (cilantro) leaves, finely chopped, to garnish

### For the spice paste

4 garlic cloves, chopped

25g/1oz fresh root ginger, chopped

4 red chillies, seeded and chopped

Per Portion Energy 276Kcal/1144kJ; Protein 12.1g; Carbohydrate 8.6g, of which sugars 8.1g; Fat 21.7g, of which saturates 3.1g; Cholesterol 126mg; Calcium 23mg; Fibre 0.3g; Sodium 674mg.

**Serves four**

8 shallots, chopped

4 garlic cloves, chopped

8–10 dried red chillies, soaked in warm water until soft, squeezed dry, seeded and chopped

5ml/1 tsp shrimp paste

30ml/2 tbsp vegetable or groundnut (peanut) oil

250ml/8fl oz/1 cup coconut cream

500g/1¼lb fresh prawns (shrimp), peeled and deveined

10ml/2 tsp tamarind paste

15ml/1 tbsp palm sugar

salt and ground black pepper

2 red chillies, seeded and finely chopped, and fresh coriander (cilantro) leaves, finely chopped, to garnish

crusty bread or steamed rice and pickles, to serve

# Sarawak *sambal udang*

Similar to the prawn *sambal goreng* of neighbouring Indonesia, this Sarawak version of the Malaysian dish *sambal udang* is simple and fiery. The Dyaks, Ibans and Melanau also cook the grubs found in sago palms in this way so, if you are travelling in Sarawak, you might want to have a good look at what is in your *sambal*! To accompany this dish, you might be offered the local, thick sago paste, a bowl of stir-fried fern shoots and a little *tuak*, the heady, home-brewed rice wine.

**1** Using a mortar and pestle or food processor, grind the shallots, garlic and dried chillies to a coarse paste. Beat in the shrimp paste.

**2** Heat the oil in a wok or heavy pan and stir in the paste until fragrant. Add the coconut cream and bubble it up until it separates. Toss in the prawns, reduce the heat and simmer for 3 minutes.

**3** Stir in the tamarind paste and the sugar and cook for a further 2 minutes until the sauce is very thick. Season with salt and pepper and scatter the chopped chillies and coriander over the top. Serve immediately with chunks of fresh, crusty bread to mop up the sauce, or with steamed rice and pickles.

**Per Portion** Energy 330Kcal/1371kJ; Protein 25.9g; Carbohydrate 3.7g, of which sugars 3.2g; Fat 23.6g, of which saturates 15.6g; Cholesterol 263mg; Calcium 156mg; Fibre 0.4g; Sodium 408mg.

# Indian dry prawn and potato curry

This delicious dish is one of the most popular curries at the Indian stalls in Singapore. Generally, in an Indian home, this curry would be served with flatbread, a yogurt dish and chutney – dry curries are easy to scoop up with the bread – but, at the *nasi kandar* stalls, it is often one of several curried dishes served with rice. It's equally delicious made with pre-cooked sweet potatoes instead of ordinary ones.

**1** Using a mortar and pestle or food processor, grind the garlic, ginger and chillies to a coarse paste. Stir in the turmeric and curry powder.

**2** Heat the ghee in a heavy pan or earthenware pot. Stir in the onion and fry until golden. Stir in the curry leaves, followed by the cinnamon stick and the spice paste. Fry until fragrant, then add the potatoes, coating them in the spices. Toss in the prawns and cook for 12 minutes. Stir in the coconut milk and bubble it up to thicken and reduce it. Season with salt and pepper to taste.

**3** Roast the fennel and mustard seeds in a small heavy pan until they begin to pop and give off a nutty aroma. Stir them into the curry and serve immediately, sprinkled with a little coriander.

### Serves four

30ml/2 tbsp ghee, or 15ml/1 tbsp vegetable oil and 15g/$^1$/$_2$oz/1 tbsp butter

1 onion, halved lengthways and sliced along the grain

a handful of fresh or dried curry leaves

1 cinnamon stick

2–3 medium-size waxy potatoes, lightly steamed, peeled and diced

500g/1$^1$/$_4$lb fresh large prawns (shrimp), peeled and deveined

200ml/7fl oz/scant 1 cup coconut milk

10ml/2 tsp fennel seeds

10ml/2 tsp brown mustard seeds

salt and ground black pepper

fresh coriander (cilantro) leaves, roughly chopped, to garnish

### For the spice paste

4 garlic cloves, chopped

25g/1oz fresh root ginger, peeled and chopped

2 red chillies, seeded and chopped

5ml/1 tsp ground turmeric

15ml/1 tbsp fish curry powder

**Per Portion** Energy 204Kcal/857kJ; Protein 23.5g; Carbohydrate 13.5g, of which sugars 5.2g; Fat 6.6g, of which saturates 0.9g; Cholesterol 244mg; Calcium 126mg; Fibre 1g; Sodium 299mg.

# Meat & poultry

# Meat & poultry

Beside the fish in the wettest part of the market the meat and poultry stalls are located, with eggs displayed in baskets and straw nearby. Slabs of raw meat are suspended from large hooks, and various cuts, such as heads, tongues, trotters and tails, are displayed on boards, while the entrails fill buckets on the floor. Because of the diverse religious customs, beef, lamb and pork are displayed separately in the markets. Next to fish and shellfish, chicken is possibly the most consumed meat, followed by pork.

For the Muslim population, which includes most of the Malays and Indonesians and some of the Peranakans and Indians, pork is *haram* (forbidden). Other meat must be *halal* – in other words, the animal's throat must be cut while the butcher recites the name of Allah. The Hindus, who make up most of the large Indian population, don't eat beef as the cow is regarded as sacred, and many of them are totally vegetarian. The Eurasians and Chinese eat just about everything; the Chinese consume very little lamb, but they make up for it by devouring almost every bit of the other animals.

## Poultry

Chicken is enjoyed across all the ethnic and religious groups, apart from the vegetarian Hindus and Buddhists. Squawking, live poultry is sold ready to be killed, plucked and jointed on the spot, or the feet are tied together and the hapless bird is taken home to its fate. The poultry section in the market displays whole quails, partridges, ducks and chickens, as well as the wings, parson's noses, giblets and feet. The most prized chickens come from the *kampung*, villages, where they roam and

**Left** *The Malays serve Hainanese chicken rice with a hot dipping sauce.*

eat freely, producing leaner, tastier meat – the equivalent of organic, free-range chickens in the West.

Chicken is the most versatile of all meats. The Chinese marinate and steam the feet; the hearts, livers and gizzards are stir-fried and offered with rice at the hawkers' stalls; the Indians make a variety of chicken curries; and the Malays are well-known for their spicy, fried chicken, *ayam goreng*, and chicken soup, *soto ayam*. Famous in Singapore is the Chinese speciality, Hainanese chicken rice, and one of the Eurasian signature dishes is chicken *Kapitan*.

Duck is consumed more by the Chinese than any other culture, although it is stewed with coriander, cooked in broths, and braised by the Malays in soy sauce.

## Pork and beef

While the Muslim communities don't eat pork, the Chinese, Peranakans and Eurasians cannot seem to get enough of it. Similarly, some of the tribal peoples of Sarawak and Sabah, such as the

Dyaks, revel in it, a favourite dish being pork stir-fried with honey. In the Chinese kitchen the fatty cuts of pork are favoured for braising, roasting and chopping up for fillings, while the ribs are stir-fried or simmered in an aromatic, peppery soup, *bak kut teh*, which the old Chinese men love to sip in the coffee shops. The pig's innards are often braised and served with noodles, and cubes of congealed pig's blood are sold in the markets.

The Peranakans and Eurasians produce a variety of festive and family pork dishes, such as *feng*, a Christmas curry that is prepared in large quantities a day in advance and served with chunks of French baguette.

*Kambing* is the Malay word for lamb, mutton, kid or goat, all of which are enjoyed at Malay, Indian, Peranakan and Eurasian tables, where the meat is generally cooked slowly in curries, or smeared in a spicy paste and roasted on a spit. The Chinese, on the other hand, enjoy beef, *daging lembu*, particularly when it is cut into thin strips and stir-fried with mushrooms, soy sauce and other sweet sauces. In the Malay kitchen beef features in traditional dishes such as *rendang*, where it is cooked in coconut milk, and *daging asam*, a sweet-sour dish of beef cooked in tamarind juice.

Beef and the meat of water buffalo feature in the cooking of the Malaysian peninsula, and wild boar and deer often end up in the pot in the wild terrains of Sabah and Sarawak.

**Serves six**

1kg/2¼lb beef topside (pot roast) or rump, cut into bitesize cubes

115g/4oz fresh coconut, grated, or desiccated (dry unsweetened shredded)

15ml/1 tbsp tamarind pulp, soaked in 90ml/6 tbsp water until soft

45ml/3 tbsp vegetable or groundnut (peanut) oil

2 onions, halved lengthways, and sliced along the grain

3 lemon grass stalks, trimmed, halved and bruised

2 cinnamon sticks

1.2 litres/2 pints/5 cups coconut milk

15ml/1 tbsp sugar

salt and ground black pepper

bread or *roti jala* and salad, to serve

## For the spice paste

8–10 dried red chillies, soaked in warm water until soft, seeded and squeezed dry

8 shallots, chopped

4–6 garlic cloves, chopped

50g/2oz fresh galangal, chopped

25g/1oz fresh turmeric, chopped

15ml/1 tbsp coriander seeds

10ml/2 tsp cumin seeds

5ml/1 tsp black peppercorns

**Slow cooking** Made with beef or the meat of water buffalo, this dish is slow-cooked to achieve the required tenderness and thickness of sauce. It is served with bread or *roti jala* (thin lacy pancakes made with coconut milk) to mop up the deliciously rich sauce, and a fresh, crunchy salad.

# Rendang

In the 15th century, when the Minangkabau people first came from Sumatra to settle in the small state of Negeri Sembilan, they brought with them their traditional social customs and fiery cooking styles. Although the customs have been diluted over time, many of the unique dishes have survived and *rendang* is one of them.

**1** First make the spice paste. Using a mortar and pestle or food processor, grind the soaked chillies, shallots, garlic, galangal and turmeric to a smooth paste. In a small heavy pan, dry-roast the coriander and cumin seeds with the peppercorns, until they give off a nutty aroma. Grind the roasted spices to a powder and stir into the spice paste. Coat the beef in the spice paste and set aside to marinate for about 1 hour.

**2** Meanwhile, dry-roast the grated coconut in a heavy pan, until it is brown and emits a nutty aroma. Using a mortar and pestle or food processor, grind the roasted coconut until it resembles brown sugar and set aside. Squeeze the tamarind to help soften it, then strain it to extract the juice. Discard the pulp.

**3** Heat the oil in a wok or heavy pan. Add the onions, lemon grass and cinnamon sticks, and fry until the onions begin to colour. Add the beef with all the spice paste and toss it around the wok, until lightly browned. Pour in the coconut milk and tamarind juice and bring to the boil, stirring all the time. Reduce the heat and simmer gently, until the sauce begins to thicken.

**4** Stir in the sugar and the ground roasted coconut, and continue to simmer very gently, stirring from time to time, until the meat is tender and the reduced sauce is very thick. This may take 2–4 hours, depending on the cut and type of meat. Season with salt and black pepper to taste, and serve hot with bread or *roti jala* and a salad.

**Per Portion** Energy 439Kcal/1842kJ; Protein 41g; Carbohydrate 19.4g, of which sugars 17.4g; Fat 22.7g, of which saturates 13.1g; Cholesterol 83mg; Calcium 94mg; Fibre 3.8g; Sodium 356mg.

# Oxtail in hot tangy sauce

Considered a delicacy in some parts of South-east Asia, oxtail and the tails of water buffalo are generally cooked for special feasts and celebrations. In Malaysia and Singapore, oxtail is cooked in European-style stews by the Eurasians and Hainanese but the Malays and Indonesians prefer to cook it slowly in a hot, tangy sauce. Served with steamed rice, or chunks of fresh, crusty bread, it makes a very tasty supper dish.

**1** Using a mortar and pestle or food processor, grind the shallots, garlic, chillies and galangal to a coarse paste. Mix the flour with the ground turmeric and spread it on a flat surface. Roll the oxtail in the flour and set aside.

**2** Heat the oil in a heavy pan or earthenware pot. Stir in the spice paste and cook until fragrant and golden. Add the oxtail joints and brown on all sides. Add the tomatoes, lemon grass stalks, lime leaves and tamarind juice. Add enough water to cover the oxtail, and bring it to the boil. Skim off any fat from the surface. Reduce the heat, put the lid on the pan and simmer the oxtail for 2 hours.

**3** Stir in the sugar, season with salt and pepper and continue to cook, uncovered, for a further 30–40 minutes, until the meat is very tender. Sprinkle with the coriander and serve straight from the pan.

**Serves four to six**

8 shallots, chopped

8 garlic cloves, chopped

4–6 red chillies, seeded and chopped

25g/1oz fresh galangal, chopped

30ml/2 tbsp rice flour or plain (all-purpose) flour

15ml/1 tbsp ground turmeric

8–12 oxtail joints, cut roughly the same size and trimmed of fat

45ml/3 tbsp vegetable oil

400g/14oz can plum tomatoes, drained

2 lemon grass stalks, halved and bruised

a handful of fresh kaffir lime leaves

225g/8oz tamarind pulp, soaked in 600ml/1 pint/2½ cups water, squeezed and strained

30–45ml/2–3 tbsp sugar

salt and ground black pepper

fresh coriander (cilantro) leaves, roughly chopped

**Per Portion** Energy 386Kcal/1611kJ; Protein 34.5g; Carbohydrate 11.3g, of which sugars 6.6g; Fat 22.6g, of which saturates 7.7g; Cholesterol 125mg; Calcium 31mg; Fibre 1.2g; Sodium 191mg.

**Serves four to six**

25g/1oz fresh root ginger, peeled and chopped

4 garlic cloves, chopped

2 red chillies, seeded and chopped

10ml/2 tsp garam masala

10ml/2 tsp ground coriander

5ml/1 tsp ground cumin

5ml/1 tsp ground turmeric

675g/1½lb lamb shoulder, cut into bitesize cubes

45ml/3 tbsp ghee, or 30ml/2 tbsp vegetable oil and 15g/½ oz/1 tbsp butter

2 onions, halved lengthways and sliced along the grain

2.5ml/½tsp sugar

4–6 cardamom pods, bruised

1 cinnamon stick

400ml/14fl oz/1⅔ cups coconut milk

salt and ground black pepper

30ml/2 tbsp roasted peanuts, crushed, and fresh coriander (cilantro) and mint leaves, coarsely chopped, to garnish

# Malay lamb *korma*

Adapted from the traditional Indian *korma*, the creamy Malay version is flavoured with coconut milk. Served at the Malay and Muslim hawker stalls, this tasty lamb *korma* is often accompanied by a fragrant rice or flatbread and a Malay salad or *sambal*.

**1** Using a mortar and pestle or food processor, grind the ginger, garlic and chillies to a paste. Stir in the garam masala, ground coriander, cumin and turmeric. Put the lamb into a shallow dish and rub the paste into it. Cover and leave to marinate for 1 hour.

**2** Heat the ghee or oil and butter in a heavy pan or earthenware pot. Add the onions and sugar, and cook until brown and almost caramelized. Stir in the cardamom pods and cinnamon stick and add the lamb with all the marinade. Mix well and cook until the meat is browned all over.

**3** Pour in the coconut milk, stir well and bring to the boil. Reduce the heat, cover the pan and cook the meat gently for 30–40 minutes until tender. Make sure the meat doesn't become dry – stir in a little extra coconut milk, or water, if necessary.

**4** Season to taste with salt and pepper. Scatter the peanuts over the top and garnish with the coriander and mint. Serve immediately.

**Per Portion** Energy 267Kcal/1117kJ; Protein 24.3g; Carbohydrate 8.5g, of which sugars 6.8g; Fat 15.4g, of which saturates 6.4g; Cholesterol 86mg; Calcium 46mg; Fibre 1.2g; Sodium 211mg.

**Serves four**

1kg/2¼lb mixed pork offal (liver, lungs, intestines and heart, optional), thoroughly cleaned and trimmed

30ml/2 tbsp vegetable oil

50g/2oz fresh root ginger, peeled and shredded

15–30ml/1–2 tbsp white wine vinegar or rice vinegar

salt

bread or steamed rice, to serve

**For the spice paste**

8 shallots, chopped

4 garlic cloves, chopped

25g/1oz fresh root ginger, peeled and chopped

30ml/2 tbsp coriander seeds

10ml/2 tsp cumin seeds

10ml/2 tsp fennel seeds

10ml/2 tsp black peppercorns

5ml/1 tsp ground turmeric

**Cooking ahead**  In most Eurasian households, a big pot of this curry is made a day in advance, as the flavours and textures improve on sitting. It is often served with French baguette and crunchy vegetables.

# Feng

The Portuguese Eurasians eat *feng* at Christmas. Traditionally made with offal, this curry represents a mix of Malay and Portuguese culinary traditions. If you are not a fan of offal, use lean pork from the hind leg – this version of the curry is popular in Singapore.

**1** First make the spice paste. Using a mortar and pestle or food processor, grind the shallots, garlic and ginger to a paste. In a heavy pan, dry-roast the coriander, cumin and fennel seeds with the peppercorns until they emit a nutty aroma. Grind the roasted spices to a powder and stir them into the spice paste with the ground turmeric.

**2** Put the offal, except for the liver, into a pan and cover with water. Bring to the boil, reduce the heat and cook for 40 minutes. Add the liver and cook for a further 5 minutes, until all the offal is tender. Drain the offal but reserve the cooking broth. Cut the offal into bitesize pieces.

**3** Heat the oil in a wok or earthenware pot. Stir in the ginger and fry until crisp. Lift the ginger out and set aside. Stir the spice paste into the oil and fry until fragrant. Add the offal and toss it to lightly brown.  Stir in the vinegar over a high heat and season. Stir in half the crispy, fried ginger and scatter the rest over the top. Serve hot with fresh, crusty bread or steamed rice.

**Per Portion** Energy 444Kcal/1858kJ; Protein 53.6g; Carbohydrate 7.2g, of which sugars 1.4g; Fat 13.3g, of which saturates 5.9g; Cholesterol 650mg; Calcium 21mg; Fibre 0.4g; Sodium 218mg.

# Pork ribs in pandanus leaves

The Malays have a penchant for sweet tastes and pork is often married with sweet flavourings in Malaysia. The Dyaks love their pork coated in honey and grilled, stir-fried or roasted. In this Chinese-style Singapore dish, the pork is marinated in honey and Western flavourings, before being wrapped in the long, thin pandanus leaves and deep-fried. Serve the pork ribs as an appetizer or as a main course with stir-fried rice or noodles.

**1** First make the marinade. Using a mortar and pestle or food processor, grind the shallots, garlic and ginger to a smooth paste. Beat in the honey, Worcestershire sauce, tomato ketchup, sour plum sauce and sesame oil. Put the pork ribs in a shallow dish and smear the marinade all over them. Set aside for 2–3 hours.

**2** Lay the pandanus leaves on a flat surface and place a marinated pork rib in the centre of each one. Tie a tight knot over each rib so that the ends poke out.

**3** Heat enough oil in a wok or heavy pan for deep-frying and fry the wrapped ribs in batches for 4–5 minutes until cooked. Serve immediately with lime wedges, allowing each diner to untie the leaves and squeeze a splash of lime over the ribs.

## Serves four to five

675g/1½lb meaty pork ribs, cut into bitesize pieces

25 pandanus (screwpine) leaves

vegetable oil, for deep-frying

2 limes, cut into wedges, to serve

### For the marinade

6 shallots, chopped

4 garlic cloves, chopped

25g/1oz fresh root ginger, peeled and chopped

30ml/2 tbsp clear honey

45ml/3 tbsp Worcestershire sauce

30ml/2 tbsp tomato ketchup

30ml/2 tbsp sour plum sauce

15ml/1 tbsp sesame oil

**Using other leaves** Pandanus leaves emit a unique fragrance but you can instead use banana or bamboo leaves cut into strips.

**Per Portion** Energy 299Kcal/1250kJ; Protein 25.5g; Carbohydrate 4.1g, of which sugars 3.8g; Fat 20.3g, of which saturates 7.3g; Cholesterol 89mg; Calcium 24mg; Fibre 0.2g; Sodium 182mg.

# Singapore five-spice meat rolls

A great favourite at the *cze cha* hawker stalls in Singapore, these deep-fried steamed rolls are delicious with a dipping sauce. Wrapped in the traditional tofu sheets, these light, tasty rolls can be served as a snack, an appetizer or as a light meal with rice and a vegetable dish or salad. Fresh tofu sheets are available in Chinese and Asian markets.

**1** Put the minced pork, chopped prawns and water chestnuts in a bowl. Add the soy sauces, sour plum sauce and sesame oil and mix well. Stir in the five-spice powder, glutinous rice flour or cornflour, and egg. Mix well.

**Serves four**

225g/8oz minced (ground) pork

150g/5oz fresh prawns (shrimp), peeled and finely chopped

115g/4oz water chestnuts, finely chopped

15ml/1 tbsp light soy sauce

15ml/1 tbsp dark soy sauce

15ml/1 tbsp sour plum sauce

7.5ml/1½ tsp sesame oil

10ml/2 tsp Chinese five-spice powder

5ml/1 tsp glutinous rice flour or cornflour (cornstarch)

1 egg, lightly beaten

4 fresh tofu sheets, 18–20cm/7–8in square, soaked in warm water

vegetable oil, for deep-frying

chilli oil, for drizzling

soy sauce mixed with chopped chillies, to serve

**2** Lay the tofu sheets on a flat surface and divide the minced pork mixture between them, placing spoonfuls towards the edge nearest you. Pull the nearest edge up over the filling, tuck in the sides and roll into a log, just like a spring roll. Moisten the last edge with a little water to seal the roll.

**3** Fill a wok one-third of the way up with water and place a bamboo steamer into it. Heat the water and place the tofu rolls in the steamer. Cover and steam for 15 minutes. Remove the steamed rolls with tongs and place them on a clean dishtowel.

**4** Heat enough oil for deep-frying in a wok. Fry the steamed rolls in batches until crisp and golden. Drain them on kitchen paper and serve whole or sliced into portions. Drizzle with chilli oil and serve with a bowl of soy sauce mixed with chopped chillies for dipping.

**Cook's tip** If you cannot find tofu sheets, try the recipe with Asian rice sheets or Middle Eastern filo pastry.

**Per Portion** Energy 339Kcal/1413kJ; Protein 24.4g; Carbohydrate 12.5g, of which sugars 2.7g; Fat 21.6g, of which saturates 4.2g; Cholesterol 158mg; Calcium 343mg; Fibre 1.2g; Sodium 665mg.

# Sarawak goat curry

Given their proximity, it is no surprise that Sarawak, Sabah and Indonesia share many dishes, although there are regional or tribal variations on a theme. One thing they all have in common is their enjoyment of mutton and goat, which they usually cook in a curry or chargrill as a spicy satay. In Sarawak, this tasty goat curry would normally be served with the local sago porridge, but it is equally delicious served with steamed jasmine rice, an Indian pilaff or chunks of fresh crusty bread and a green mango or papaya salad.

**1** First make the spice paste. Using a mortar and pestle or food processor, grind the shallots, garlic, chillies, galangal, turmeric, lemon grass and nuts to a coarse paste. Grind the coriander and cumin seeds separately and stir them into the spice paste.

**2** Heat the oil in a wok and stir in the spice paste with the cinnamon sticks. Once they start to emit a fragrant aroma, add the strips of goat, tossing them around the wok to brown them lightly. Stir in the tomatoes with the sugar and cook for 2 minutes before pouring in the coconut milk. Bring to the boil, stir in the lime leaves and reduce the heat.

**3** Cover and simmer gently for about 1$^{1}/_{2}$ hours, until the meat is tender. Add more coconut milk if necessary to prevent the curry becoming too dry. Season to taste with salt, sprinkle with coriander and serve with chillies and bread.

**Serves four**

30ml/2 tbsp vegetable or groundnut (peanut) oil

2 cinnamon sticks

1 kg/2$^{1}/_{4}$lb lean goat meat, from the leg or shoulder, cut into bitesize strips

4 tomatoes, skinned, seeded and chopped

15–30ml/1–2 tbsp palm sugar

900ml/1$^{1}/_{2}$ pints/3$^{3}/_{4}$ cups coconut milk

a handful of kaffir lime leaves

salt

fresh coriander (cilantro) leaves, roughly chopped, to garnish

3–4 green chillies, seeded and quartered lengthways, and bread, to serve

## For the spice paste

8 shallots, chopped

6 garlic cloves, chopped

4 red chillies, seeded and chopped

50g/2oz galangal, chopped

25g/1oz fresh turmeric, chopped

2 lemon grass stalks, trimmed and chopped

4 candlenuts or macadamia nuts

15ml/1 tbsp coriander seeds

5ml/1 tsp cumin seeds

**Per Portion** Energy 625Kcal/2614kJ; Protein 51.3g; Carbohydrate 19.8g, of which sugars 19.2g; Fat 38.5g, of which saturates 14.7g; Cholesterol 190mg; Calcium 126mg; Fibre 2g; Sodium 488mg.

# Malaysian fried chicken

You cannot visit Malaysia or Singapore without trying the famous fried chicken. Indonesian in origin, *ayam goreng* puts Western fried chicken to shame. First the chicken is cooked in spices and flavourings to ensure a depth of taste, then it is simply deep-fried to form a crisp, golden skin.

**1** Using a mortar and pestle or food processor, grind the shallots, garlic, ginger or galangal, turmeric and lemon grass to a paste.

**2** Place the chicken pieces in a heavy pan or earthenware pot and smear with the spice paste. Add the *kecap manis* and 150ml/¼ pint/⅔ cup water. Bring to the boil, reduce the heat and cook the chicken for about 25 minutes, turning it from time to time, until the liquid has evaporated. The chicken should be dry before deep-frying, but the spices should be sticking to it. Season with salt and pepper.

**3** Heat enough oil for deep-frying in a wok. Fry the chicken pieces in batches until golden brown and crisp. Drain them on kitchen paper and serve hot.

**Serves four**

2 shallots, chopped

4 garlic cloves, chopped

50g/2oz fresh root ginger or galangal, peeled and chopped

25g/1oz fresh turmeric, chopped

2 lemon grass stalks, chopped

12 chicken thighs or drumsticks or 6 whole chicken legs, separated into drumsticks and thighs

30ml/2 tbsp *kecap manis*

salt and ground black pepper

vegetable oil, for deep-frying

**To serve** Served with a *sambal*, or pickle, *agam goreng* makes a delicious snack, but for a main course, serve with yellow or fragrant coconut rice and a salad. If you cannot find *kecap manis*, use soy sauce sweetened with palm sugar, available in Chinese and Asian markets, or substitute the same quantity of dark soy sauce and 15ml/1 tbsp sugar.

**Per Portion** Energy 396Kcal/1639kJ; Protein 27g; Carbohydrate 1.5g, of which sugars 1.1g; Fat 31.3g, of which saturates 6.8g; Cholesterol 150mg; Calcium 38mg; Fibre 0.2g; Sodium 358mg.

# Hainanese chicken rice

**Serves four to six**

1 chicken (1.25kg/2$\frac{1}{2}$lb), cleaned

30ml/2 tbsp light soy sauce

15ml/1 tbsp Chinese rice wine

50g/2oz fresh root ginger, peeled, thickly sliced and crushed

4 garlic cloves, lightly crushed

2 spring onions (scallions), crushed

1.5 litres/2$\frac{1}{2}$ pints/6$\frac{1}{4}$ cups chicken stock

10ml/2 tsp sesame oil

225g/8oz/generous 1 cup jasmine rice, rinsed and drained

salt and ground black pepper

## For the *sambal*

10 red chillies, seeded and chopped

6 garlic cloves, chopped

25g/1oz fresh root ginger, peeled and chopped

15ml/1 tbsp sesame or groundnut (peanut) oil

15–30ml/1–2 tbsp fresh lime juice

10ml/2 tsp sugar

2.5ml/$\frac{1}{2}$ tsp salt

## For the garnish

fresh coriander (cilantro) leaves

dark soy sauce

1 small cucumber, halved lengthways and finely sliced

3 spring onions, trimmed and sliced

This Hainanese-derived recipe focuses on an unusual steeping process to ensure smooth, silky chicken, which is accompanied by aromatic rice, a bowl of chicken broth, soy sauce for dipping and a garnish of crunchy spring onions and cucumber. With their preference for hot tastes, the Malays add a pungent ginger and chilli dipping sauce.

**1** Rub the chicken, inside and out, with 15ml/1 tbsp soy sauce and the rice wine. Place the ginger, garlic and spring onions in the cavity. Leave to stand for 30 minutes.

**2** Bring the stock to the boil in a deep pan. Immerse the chicken in the stock. Bring back to the boil, cover the pan and turn off the heat. Leave the chicken to steep for 15 minutes. Lift the chicken to drain the cavity, reheat the stock to boiling point, cover the pan and steep the chicken off the heat for a further 15 minutes. Repeat the process every 15 minutes, until the chicken has steeped for 1 hour.

**3** Lift the chicken out of the stock, allowing the juices to drip back into the pan, and plunge it into a bowl of iced water. Bring the stock back to the boil. Drain the chicken, trim off the wings, neck and legs, and add to the stock. Rub the remaining 15ml/1 tbsp soy sauce and the sesame oil over the chicken and set aside.

**4** Keep the stock simmering, skim off any fat and season. Measure 550ml/18fl oz/2$\frac{1}{2}$ cups of the stock and pour into a separate pan (cover the remaining stock and keep it barely simmering). Bring the measured stock to the boil and add the rice. Stir once, reduce the heat and simmer until the stock is absorbed. Turn off the heat, cover the pan with a dishtowel, then the lid, and leave to stand for 15 minutes.

**5** Meanwhile, prepare the *sambal*. Using a mortar and pestle or food processor, grind the chillies, garlic and ginger to a smooth paste. Bind with the oil and lime juice, and stir in the sugar and salt. Spoon the *sambal* into individual dipping bowls.

**6** To serve, first joint the chicken. Remove the skin and separate the meat from the bones. Slice the thighs and breasts into bitesize pieces. Place the chicken on a platter and garnish with a few coriander leaves. Pack spoonfuls of the rice into a small bowl and invert it on to each plate, so that each person is given a mound of rice. Place the bowls of *sambal* on each plate, along with individual bowls of dark soy sauce, slices of cucumber and a few coriander leaves.

**7** Ladle the hot chicken broth into warmed serving bowls and sprinkle spring onions over the top. Place a plate of rice and sauces, and bowl of broth, in front of each person, and set the chicken in the middle of the table. Use chopsticks to eat, dipping a piece of chicken with some rice into one of the sauces. The broth is sipped or spooned over the rice.

**Per Portion** Energy 460Kcal/1913kJ; Protein 28.6g; Carbohydrate 30.4g, of which sugars 0.4g; Fat 24.6g, of which saturates 6.7g; Cholesterol 133mg; Calcium 37mg; Fibre 0.5g; Sodium 108mg.

# Curry *Kapitan* with coconut and chilli relish

Curry *Kapitan* recalls the traditional role of the Chinese *Kapitan*, a man of considerable social standing among the Malay and Chinese people in old Melaka. It is said to be a dish invented by the Peranakans, perhaps to present to the *Kapitan* or to celebrate his role. A chicken curry, made with coconut milk, it spans the spectrum of the inhabitants of old Melaka through its use of spices and flavourings – Chinese, Malay, Portuguese and Indian – and could be regarded as Melaka in a pot.

**1** First make the *rempah*. Using a mortar and pestle or food processor, grind the chillies, shallots, garlic and ginger to a paste. Beat in the shrimp paste and stir in the dried spices.

**2** Soak the tamarind pulp in 150ml/¼ pint/⅔ cup warm water until soft. Squeeze the pulp to soften it, then strain the pulp to extract the juice. Discard the pulp.

**3** In a heavy pan, roast half the grated coconut until it is brown and emits a nutty aroma. Using a mortar and pestle or food processor, grind the roasted coconut until it resembles sugar grains – this is called *kerisik*.

**4** Heat the oil in a wok or earthenware pot, and stir in the *rempah* and cinnamon sticks until fragrant. Add the chicken strips. Pour in the coconut milk and tamarind water, and stir in the sugar. Reduce the heat and cook gently for about 10 minutes. Stir in half the ground roasted coconut to thicken the sauce and season.

**5** In a bowl, mix the remaining grated coconut with the chillies, coriander and juice of 1 lime to serve as a relish. Cut the other lime into wedges. Spoon the chicken curry into a serving dish and garnish with a few coriander leaves. Serve with the coconut and chilli relish, the lime wedges to squeeze over it and a bowl of steamed rice.

### Serves four

#### For the *rempah* spice paste

6–8 dried red chillies, soaked in warm water until soft, seeded and squeezed dry

6–8 shallots, chopped

4–6 garlic cloves, chopped

25g/1oz fresh root ginger, chopped

5ml/1 tsp shrimp paste

10ml/2 tsp ground turmeric

10ml/2 tsp Chinese five-spice powder

#### For the curry

15–30ml/1–2 tbsp tamarind pulp

1 fresh coconut, grated (shredded)

30–45ml/2–3 tbsp vegetable or groundnut (peanut) oil

1–2 cinnamon sticks

12 chicken thighs, boned and cut into bitesize strips lengthways

600ml/1 pint/2½ cups coconut milk

15ml/1 tbsp palm sugar

salt and ground black pepper

#### For the relish

1 green chilli, seeded and finely sliced

1 red chilli, seeded and finely sliced

fresh coriander (cilantro) leaves, finely chopped (reserve a few leaves for garnishing)

2 limes

steamed rice, to serve

**Cook's tip** The palm sugar lends its unique sweet, caramelized flavour to the dish. As a substitute, you could try muscovado sugar.

**Per Portion** Energy 487Kcal/2024kJ; Protein 29.2g; Carbohydrate 11.3g, of which sugars 10.6g; Fat 36.4g, of which saturates 19.2g; Cholesterol 150mg; Calcium 114mg; Fibre 4.4g; Sodium 267mg.

## Devil's Curry

This Eurasian dish known as curry *Debal* or Devil's curry really is devilishly hot. Every Eurasian household has its own version of this chicken and vegetable hotpot in a fiery, sour sauce. Served as a meal on its own with bread to mop up the sauce, it is often cooked at family celebrations.

**1** First make the spice paste. Using a mortar and pestle or food processor, grind the chillies, shallots, garlic, ginger and nuts to a paste. Stir in the turmeric and set aside.

**2** Mix together the ingredients for the marinade and rub it into the chicken pieces. Leave to marinate for 30 minutes.

**3** Heat the oil in a wok or heavy pan. Stir in the onion, ginger and garlic and fry until golden. Add the spice paste and stir until fragrant. Toss in the marinated chicken and stir until it begins to brown, then pour in enough water to cover.

**4** Bring to the boil and add the vinegar, sugar and potatoes. Reduce the heat and cook gently until the potatoes are tender. Add the courgettes and cook for 2 minutes, then stir in the cabbage. Stir in the mustard paste and season with salt. Serve hot with bread or chill overnight to allow the flavours to mingle, then reheat the next day.

### Serves six

4–6 chicken breasts or 12 boned chicken thighs, cut into bitesize chunks

60ml/4 tbsp vegetable oil

1 onion, halved lengthways, and sliced along the grain

25g/1oz fresh root ginger, peeled and cut into julienne strips

4 garlic cloves, cut into strips

30–45ml/2–3 tbsp vinegar

10ml/2 tsp sugar

3 medium potatoes, cut into bitesize chunks

2 courgettes (zucchini), partially peeled, halved lengthways, seeded and cut into bitesize chunks

8 Chinese leaves (Chinese cabbage), cut into bitesize squares

10ml/2 tsp brown mustard seeds, ground and mixed to a paste with a little water

salt

fresh crusty bread, to serve

### For the spice paste

10 dried chillies, soaked in warm water until soft, seeded and squeezed dry

6 fresh red chillies, seeded and chopped

8 shallots, chopped

6 garlic cloves, chopped

25g/1oz fresh root ginger, peeled and chopped

6 candlenuts or macadamia nuts

10ml/2 tsp ground turmeric

### For the marinade

15ml/1 tbsp light soy sauce

15ml/1 tbsp dark soy sauce

10ml/2 tsp rice or white wine vinegar

10ml/2 tsp sugar

**Per Portion** Energy 270Kcal/1136kJ; Protein 32.5g; Carbohydrate 15.4g, of which sugars 4.6g; Fat 9.1g, of which saturates 1.3g; Cholesterol 88mg; Calcium 36mg; Fibre 1.8g; Sodium 441mg.

# Malay braised duck in aromatic soy sauce

The Chinese communities in Malaysia and Singapore often braise duck, goose, chicken or pork in soy sauce and warm flavourings, such as star anise and cinnamon. Such dishes are found at Chinese hawker stalls and coffee shops, and there are many variations on the theme. The Malays like to add turmeric and lemon grass to the flavourings and, to achieve their desired fiery kick, chillies are always tucked into the recipe somewhere.

**Serves four to six**

1 duck (about 2kg/4½lb), washed and trimmed

15–30ml/1–2 tbsp Chinese five-spice powder

25g/1oz fresh turmeric, chopped

25g/1oz galangal, chopped

4 garlic cloves, chopped

30ml/2 tbsp sesame oil

12 shallots, peeled and left whole

2–3 lemon grass stalks, halved and lightly crushed

4 cinnamon sticks

8 star anise

12 cloves

600ml/1 pint/2½ cups light soy sauce

120ml/4fl oz/½ cup dark soy sauce

30–45ml/2–3 tbsp palm sugar

fresh coriander (cilantro) leaves, 2 green and 2 red chillies, seeded and quartered lengthways, to garnish

steamed jasmine rice and salad, to serve

**1** Rub the duck, inside and out, with the five-spice powder and place in the refrigerator, uncovered, for 6–8 hours.

**2** Using a mortar and pestle or food processor, grind the turmeric, galangal and garlic to a smooth paste. Heat the oil in a heavy pan and stir in the spice paste until it becomes fragrant. Stir in the shallots, lemon grass, cinnamon sticks, star anise and cloves. Pour in the soy sauces and stir in the sugar until dissolved.

**3** Place the duck in the pan, baste with the sauce, and add 550ml/18fl oz/2½ cups water. Bring to the boil, reduce the heat and cover the pan. Simmer gently for 4–6 hours, basting from time to time, until the duck is very tender. Garnish with coriander and chillies, and serve with rice and salad.

**Per Portion** Energy 119Kcal/498kJ; Protein 10.2g; Carbohydrate 4.6g, of which sugars 3.4g; Fat 6.9g, of which saturates 1.5g; Cholesterol 50mg; Calcium 35mg; Fibre 1.1g; Sodium 412mg.

# Vegetables & salads

# Vegetables & salads

Shopping for vegetables and fruit is an everyday activity for most cooks. In rural Malaysia, makeshift stalls are set up to sell local vegetables and fruit, but most people head to the wet markets. Every day, vegetables and fruit are brought over the causeway into Singapore, as it is fully dependent on Malaysia for its agricultural produce and water. As the wet markets fill up, the stalls begin to transform into a maze of colour and bustling activity.

While the fruit stalls, often erected at one end of the market, are loaded with bananas, pineapples, oranges, mangoes and furry red rambutans, the vegetable stalls at the other end pile up with water chestnuts, exotic tubers, aubergines (eggplants), gourds, bamboo shoots and beansprouts. When you enter the big wet markets the display of vegetables is breathtaking, including several not home-grown, such as apples from China, and potatoes and tomatoes from Australia.

## Vegetables

The local vegetables include the long green bitter gourd, which the Malays slice thinly and stir-fry with prawns (shrimp) and the Chinese stuff with a fish paste. Juicy yam beans are added to salads, or cooked in fillings for pastries and *popiah*. The ever-popular water spinach, *kangkung*, with its large arrow-shaped leaves, is invariably served with *sambal belacan*. A range of cabbages is popular, including salted mustard cabbage, with its sour-tasting leaves that Eurasians and Peranakans use in their soups, and which the Malays add to some of their curries. Another favourite is the elongated or round

**Left** *Dried shrimp add flavour to this spicy stir-fried* kangkung *dish.*

**Left** *Firm tofu may be cut into slices or cubes and stir-fried or deep-fried.*

winter melon, also known as wax gourd, which the Chinese hollow out and use as a steaming vessel for soup, and the Malays cook with sugar to make winter melon candy. Short, thick cucumbers with variegated skin are ideal for pickles, garnishes and salads. *Bunga telang*, blue pea flowers, are not actually used as vegetables but are boiled in water and squeezed to extract the natural dye which gives the Kelantan *nasi kerabu* its unique bluish tinge. This dye is also used in a number of Malay, Peranakan, and Eurasian dishes.

In general, most vegetable dishes and salads are presented as side dishes to accompany the rice or the main dish and grilled meats. Some vegetable dishes are served as meals on their own, particularly among vegetarian Indians who produce exciting dishes that combine Indian and Malay styles. Crisp salads and raw pickled vegetables often accompany grilled meats and fish, and the Indonesian and Malay specialities,

such as *rojak* and *kerabu,* are served as snacks at hawker stalls.

The recipes in this section can be served as side or main dishes by adjusting the quantities, and can be served with dishes of your choice, following the flexible Malay approach of mixing styles on one plate.

## Soya bean products

Similar to other regions of South-east Asia, the protein-rich by-products of soya beans are used in Malaysia and Singapore. Tofu, fermented beans and soy sauce find their way into many dishes on a daily basis. Tofu comes in various forms: *taofu* or *tauhu* is the "silken" variety, which is added to soups, or sliced and stir-fried with egg or

minced (ground) pork; the firmer blocks of tofu are stir-fried in a number of dishes, or deep-fried and added to salads. The firmest variety of tofu, *taukua*, is split open to form a pocket, which is often stuffed with vegetables and pieces of braised duck. The Chinese and Peranakans also make tofu sheets, *taukee*, from the skin that forms on the surface of the tofu as it is made. Using tongs or chopsticks the skin is lifted off and dried flat, until it can be folded and stored. Before use, the skins need to be soaked in warm water to make them pliable for wrapping. The Indonesian staple, *tempeh*, is regarded as a nutritious food and is enjoyed for its crunchy texture and nutty flavour when stir-fried and served hot with *nasi lemak*. It consists of boiled soya beans, sprinkled with yeast and packed into blocks that are wrapped in banana leaves and left to ferment.

**Right** *A mixture of fruit and vegetables, including bananas, dried mushrooms, yard long beans, bamboo shoots, banana leaves, and in the background mangoes, limes and a durian.*

# Stir-fried spicy *kangkung* with dried shrimp

*Kangkung* is the Malay name for water spinach, or morning glory, which is a wonderful green vegetable with spear-shaped leaves. The versatility of water spinach is much appreciated throughout South-east Asia, where it is used in soups, fillings and braised dishes, or simply stir-fried on its own. This dish serves two as a main dish or four as a side dish.

**Serves two to four**

4 garlic cloves, chopped

25g/1oz fresh root ginger, peeled and chopped

2 red chillies, seeded and chopped

30ml/2 tbsp dried shrimp, soaked in warm water to soften and drained

5ml/1 tsp shrimp paste

30ml/2 tbsp vegetable or groundnut (peanut) oil

7.5ml/1½ tsp palm sugar

15–30ml/1–2 tbsp light soy sauce

500g/1¼lb fresh *kangkung* or water spinach leaves, washed and trimmed

salt and ground black pepper

1 red chilli, seeded and sliced, to garnish

**Cook's tip** Bundles of water spinach are available in Chinese markets but you could replace it with ordinary garden spinach. Serve as a snack with bread and sliced chillies or as a side dish to accompany grilled or fried meats.

**1** Using a mortar and pestle or food processor, grind the garlic, ginger and chillies to a smooth paste. Add the dried shrimp and grind them to a paste. Beat in the shrimp paste and bind with a little of the oil.

**2** Heat the rest of the oil in a wok or heavy pan. Stir in the spicy shrimp paste and cook over a low heat for 2–3 minutes until fragrant and beginning to colour. Stir in the sugar and soy sauce until well mixed.

**3** Add the *kankung*, tossing it around the pan to coat the leaves in the spicy juices. Cover with the lid for a few minutes to let the leaves wilt in the steam, then toss them around once more. Season to taste with salt and pepper, scatter the red chilli over the top and serve immediately.

**Per Portion** Energy 107Kcal/441kJ; Protein 7.7g; Carbohydrate 4g, of which sugars 3.8g; Fat 6.7g, of which saturates 0.8g; Cholesterol 38mg; Calcium 304mg; Fibre 2.6g; Sodium 500mg.

# Sarawak aubergines with lemon grass and coconut milk

One of the treasures of Sarawak is the round, orange aubergine grown by Dyak farmers, which is pretty to look at and delicate in flavour. It is particularly tasty cooked in coconut milk with lots of chillies, ginger and lemon grass. The Dyaks serve it with their local staple, sago porridge, and a handful of fresh chillies for that extra bit of fire, but it is delicious with plain jasmine or coconut rice and/or chunks of crusty bread.

**1** First make the spice paste. Using a mortar and pestle or food processor, grind the chillies, garlic, shallots, ginger and lemon grass to a coarse paste. Grind in the dried shrimp and beat in the shrimp paste.

**2** Mix the turmeric and chilli powder together. Rub the mixture all over the aubergine wedges. Heat the oil in a wok or heavy pan. Stir in the spice paste and lemon grass. Add the aubergine wedges, and cook until lightly browned. Pour in the coconut milk, stir well, and bubble it up to thicken. Reduce the heat and cook gently for 15–20 minutes until the aubergine is tender but not mushy. Season with salt and pepper to taste. Sprinkle the coriander over the top and serve straight from the wok with the extra chillies to munch on, if you like. Serve with jasmine or coconut rice.

### Serves four

15ml/1 tbsp ground turmeric

5ml/1 tsp chilli powder

3 slender orange aubergines (eggplants) or 8 baby aubergines, cut in wedges

45ml/3 tbsp vegetable or groundnut (peanut) oil

2 lemon grass stalks, trimmed, halved and bruised

600ml/1 pint/2½ cups coconut milk

salt and ground black pepper

a small bunch fresh coriander (cilantro), roughly chopped, to garnish

jasmine or coconut rice and 2 green chillies, seeded and quartered lengthways (optional), to serve

### For the spice paste

4–6 dried red chillies, soaked in warm water until soft, squeezed dry and seeded

4 garlic cloves, chopped

4 shallots, chopped

25g/1oz fresh root ginger, peeled and chopped

2 lemon grass stalks, trimmed and chopped

30ml/2 tbsp dried shrimp, re-hydrated in warm water and drained

5ml/1 tsp shrimp paste

**Variation** If you cannot find these orange aubergines, use purple ones.

**Per Portion** Energy 154Kcal/644kJ; Protein 6.2g; Carbohydrate 11.9g, of which sugars 11g; Fat 9.5g, of which saturates 1.4g; Cholesterol 38mg; Calcium 175mg; Fibre 3g; Sodium 497mg.

**Serves two to four**

6 shallots, chopped

4 garlic cloves, chopped

2 red chillies, seeded and chopped

1 lemon grass stalk, trimmed and chopped

5ml/1 tsp shrimp paste

15ml/1 tbsp sesame oil

15–30ml/1–2 tbsp soy sauce

7.5ml/1½ tsp sugar

2 slender, purple aubergines (eggplants), partially peeled in strips and halved lengthways

vegetable oil, for deep-frying

## To garnish

1 green chilli, seeded and finely chopped

a small bunch each of fresh mint and coriander (cilantro), stalks removed, finely chopped

# Deep-fried aubergine with spicy garlic sauce

This dish, *terung sambal*, is often served at the rice stalls in Singapore as an accompaniment to a main rice dish such as *nasi lemak*, Malay coconut rice. Many cooks at the stalls, and in the home, make up batches of different sambals to be stored and used for quick dishes like this one. Generally, the aubergines are deep-fried at the hawker stalls, but you could bake them in the oven at home. Serve *terung sambal* as a snack with bread or as a side dish to rice or grilled meats.

**1** Using a mortar and pestle or food processor, grind the shallots, garlic, chillies and lemon grass to a paste. Beat in the shrimp paste and mix well.

**2** Heat the sesame oil in a small wok or heavy pan. Stir in the spice paste and cook until fragrant and brown. Stir in the soy sauce and sugar and cook until smooth. Remove from the heat.

**3** Heat enough oil for deep-frying in a wok or heavy pan. Drop in the aubergine halves and fry until tender. Drain on kitchen paper, then press down the centre of each half to make a dip or shallow pouch. Arrange the aubergine halves on a plate and smear with the spicy sauce. Garnish with the chopped green chilli, mint and coriander and serve at room temperature.

**Per Portion** Energy 158Kcal/654kJ; Protein 1.6g; Carbohydrate 6.5g, of which sugars 5.1g; Fat 14.2g, of which saturates 1.8g; Cholesterol 0mg; Calcium 24mg; Fibre 2.7g; Sodium 271mg.

**Serves four**

4 shallots, chopped

2 garlic cloves, chopped

1 lemon grass stalk, trimmed and chopped

25g/1oz fresh root ginger, peeled and chopped

2 red chillies, seeded and chopped

5ml/1 tsp shrimp paste

5ml/1 tsp turmeric powder

5ml/1 tsp palm sugar

15ml/1 tbsp sesame or groundnut (peanut) oil

400ml/14fl oz/1²/₃ cups coconut milk

450g/1lb Chinese leaves (Chinese cabbage) or kale, cut into thick ribbons, or pak choi (bok choy), separated into leaves, or a mixture of the two

salt and ground black pepper

# Nonya cabbage in coconut milk

In Melaka and Johor, where the culinary culture is influenced by the Chinese, Malay, and Peranakans, it is no wonder that Nonya cuisine blooms. With good agricultural ground, there is an abundance of vegetables which, in this part of Malaysia, are often cooked in coconut milk. For this dish, you could use green beans, curly kale, or any type of cabbage, all of which are delicious served with steamed, braised or grilled fish dishes.

**1** Using a mortar and pestle or food processor, grind the shallots, garlic, lemon grass, ginger and chillies to a paste. Beat in the shrimp paste, turmeric and sugar.

**2** Heat the oil in a wok or heavy pan, and stir in the spice paste. Cook until fragrant and beginning to colour. Pour in the coconut milk, mix well, and bubble it up to thicken. Drop in the cabbage leaves, coating them in the coconut milk, and cook for a minute or two until wilted. Season to taste and serve immediately.

**Per Portion** Energy 112Kcal/469kJ; Protein 2.1g; Carbohydrate 13g, of which sugars 12.6g; Fat 6.1g, of which saturates 1g; Cholesterol 0mg; Calcium 89mg; Fibre 2.6g; Sodium 119mg.

**Serves four**

6 garlic cloves, chopped

25g/1oz fresh root ginger, peeled and chopped

30ml/2 tbsp ghee, or 15ml/1 tbsp oil and 15g/$^1$/$_2$oz/1 tbsp butter

6 shallots, halved lengthways and sliced along the grain

2 green chillies, seeded and finely sliced

10ml/2 tsp sugar

a handful of fresh or dried curry leaves

2 cinnamon sticks

5–10ml/1–2 tsp ground turmeric

15ml/1 tbsp garam masala

500g/1$^1$/$_4$lb waxy potatoes, cut into bitesize pieces

2 tomatoes, peeled, seeded and quartered

250ml/8fl oz/1 cup Greek (US strained plain) yogurt

salt and ground black pepper

5ml/1 tsp red chilli powder, and fresh coriander (cilantro) and mint leaves, finely chopped, to garnish

1 lemon, quartered, to serve

# Potato curry with yogurt

Variations of this simple Indian curry are popular at the Malay and Muslim stalls, and at the *roti* stalls, where it is served with flatbread. Some of the Singapore coffee shops even serve it for breakfast. Generally, the Malays and Indians serve this dish with a meat curry and rice, but it is also delicious on its own, served with yogurt and a spicy pickle or chutney. A dry version, without yogurt, is used as a filling for some of the tasty flatbreads and savoury pastries sold at the hawker stalls in Singapore.

**1** Using a mortar and pestle or a food processor, grind the garlic and ginger to a coarse paste. Heat the ghee in a heavy pan and stir in the shallots and chillies, until fragrant. Add the garlic and ginger paste with the sugar, and stir until the mixture begins to colour. Stir in the curry leaves, cinnamon sticks, turmeric and garam masala, and toss in the potatoes, making sure they are coated in the spice mixture.

**2** Pour in just enough cold water to cover the potatoes. Bring to the boil, then reduce the heat and simmer until the potatoes are just cooked – they should still have a bite to them.

**3** Season with salt and pepper to taste. Gently toss in the tomatoes to heat them through. Fold in the yogurt so that it is streaky rather than completely mixed in. Sprinkle with the chilli powder, coriander and mint. Serve immediately from the pan, with lemon to squeeze over it and flatbread for scooping it up.

**Variation** This recipe also works well with sweet potatoes, butternut squash or pumpkin, all of which absorb the flavours.

**Per Portion** Energy 231Kcal/967kJ; Protein 6.7g; Carbohydrate 26.2g, of which sugars 7.4g; Fat 12.4g, of which saturates 4.1g; Cholesterol 0mg; Calcium 110mg; Fibre 2g; Sodium 63mg.

# Roasted vegetables with a peanut sauce

Served as a vegetable side dish or as a main course, a selection of blanched, fried, grilled or roasted vegetables in a peanut sauce, enhanced by the usual chillies, soy sauce and other flavourings, is a great favourite throughout South-east Asia. The idea was probably introduced to southern Malaysia and Singapore from Indonesia, and the dish has become widely popular, especially among the Malays and Peranakans, who often serve it as a snack with bread, or as one of the dishes at the *cze cha* stalls, along with boiled eggs, deep-fried tofu, green chillies stuffed with fish paste, pickles and rice.

**1** Preheat the oven to 200°C/400°F/Gas 6. Arrange the vegetables in a shallow oven dish. Using a mortar and pestle or food processor, grind the garlic and ginger to a paste, and smear it over the vegetables. Sprinkle with a little salt and pour over the oil. Place the dish in the oven for about 45 minutes, until the vegetables are tender and slightly browned – toss them in the oil halfway through cooking.

**2** Meanwhile, make the sauce. Using a mortar and pestle or food processor, grind the garlic and chillies to a paste. Beat in the shrimp paste and peanuts. Stir in the soy sauce, lime juice, vinegar and sugar or honey, and blend with a little water so that the sauce is the consistency of pouring cream. Season with salt and pepper and adjust the sweet and sour balance to taste.

**3** Arrange the roasted vegetables on a plate. Drizzle the sauce over them, or serve it separately in a bowl. Sprinkle the ground peanuts over the top and serve warm, or at room temperature, with fresh crusty bread to mop up the garlicky peanut sauce.

**Serves four**

1 long, slender aubergine (eggplant), partially peeled and cut into long strips

2 courgettes (zucchini), partially peeled and cut into long strips

1 thick, long sweet potato, cut into long strips

2 leeks, trimmed, halved widthways and lengthways

2 garlic cloves, chopped

25g/1oz fresh root ginger, peeled and chopped

60ml/4 tbsp vegetable or groundnut (peanut) oil

salt

fresh crusty bread, to serve

**For the sauce**

4 garlic cloves, chopped

2–3 red chillies, seeded and chopped

5ml/1 tsp shrimp paste

115g/4oz/1 cup roasted peanuts, crushed

15–30ml/1–2 tbsp dark soy sauce

juice of 1 lime

5–10ml/1–2 tsp Chinese rice vinegar

10ml/2 tsp palm sugar or clear honey

salt and ground black pepper

**For the garnish**

30ml/3 tbsp roasted peanuts, ground

**Per Portion** Energy 361Kcal/1502kJ; Protein 11.9g; Carbohydrate 22.7g, of which sugars 11.1g; Fat 25.4g, of which saturates 4.1g; Cholesterol 0mg; Calcium 76mg; Fibre 6.9g; Sodium 292mg.

## Winter melon *pachadi*

In southern India, there are a variety of *pachadi* and *raita* dishes designed to cool the palate and aid digestion when eating hot, spicy food. Yogurt-based, these dishes are made with cooling vegetables and herbs, such as winter melon, okra, courgette, spinach, pumpkin, and cucumber with mint, which is the refreshing combination found in cucumber *raita*.

**1** Put the winter melon in a heavy pan with the turmeric and chilli powder and pour in enough water to just cover. Bring to the boil and cook gently, uncovered, until the winter melon is tender and all the water has evaporated.

**2** In a bowl, beat the yogurt with the salt and sugar until smooth and creamy. Add the ginger and green chilli, and fold in the warm winter melon.

**3** Heat the oil in small heavy pan. Stir in the asafoetida and the mustard seeds. As soon as the mustard seeds begin to pop, stir in the curry leaves and dried chilli. When the chilli darkens, add the spices to the yogurt and mix thoroughly. Serve at room temperature.

**Serves four**

225g/8oz winter melon, peeled, seeded and diced

5ml/1 tsp ground turmeric

5ml/1 tsp red chilli powder

300ml/$^1$/$_2$ pint/1$^1$/$_4$ cups Greek (US strained plain) yogurt

2.5ml/$^1$/$_2$ tsp salt

2.5ml/$^1$/$_2$ tsp sugar

15g/$^1$/$_2$oz fresh root ginger, peeled and grated

1 green chilli, seeded and finely chopped

15ml/1 tbsp vegetable oil

1.5ml/$^1$/$_4$ tsp ground asafoetida

5ml/1 tsp brown mustard seeds

8–10 dried curry leaves

1 dried red chilli, seeded and roughly chopped

**Cook's tip** In Malaysia and Singapore cooling Indian dishes like *pachadi* are often served at the Indian and Malay stalls and coffee shops to balance the hot curries and spicy grilled dishes. In many Indian households, the *pachadi* is made a day or two in advance, so that the flavours mingle.

**Per Portion** Energy 127Kcal/527kJ; Protein 5.1g; Carbohydrate 5.3g, of which sugars 5.3g; Fat 10.5g, of which saturates 4.2g; Cholesterol 0mg; Calcium 120mg; Fibre 0.2g; Sodium 316mg.

# Cucumber and shallot salad

In Malaysia and Singapore, this light, refreshing salad is served with Indian food almost as often as the cooling mint-flavoured cucumber *raita*. The Malays also enjoy this salad with many of their spicy fish and grilled meat dishes. It can be made ahead of time and kept in the refrigerator. Serve it as a salad, or a relish.

**1** Slice the cucumber halves finely and sprinkle with salt. Set aside for about 15 minutes. Rinse well and drain off any excess water.

**2** Put the cucumber, shallots and chillies in a bowl. Pour in the coconut milk and toss well. Sprinkle most of the roasted cumin over the top. Just before serving, toss the salad again, season with salt, and sprinkle the rest of the roasted cumin over the top. Serve with lime wedges to squeeze over the salad.

**Serves four**

1 cucumber, peeled, halved lengthways and seeded

4 shallots, halved lengthways and sliced finely along the grain

1–2 green chillies, seeded and sliced finely lengthways

60ml/4 tbsp coconut milk

5–10ml/1–2 tsp cumin seeds, dry-roasted and ground to a powder

salt

1 lime, quartered, to serve

**Per Portion** Energy 17Kcal/68kJ; Protein 0.7g; Carbohydrate 3.3g, of which sugars 2.7g; Fat 0.1g, of which saturates 0g; Cholesterol 0mg; Calcium 19mg; Fibre 0.7g; Sodium 15mg.

## *Avial* with roasted coconut

Originally from southern India, this delicious dish has found its way into many Malay homes. In Singapore, it is served in some coffee shops and at the Indian and Malay stalls, where it is often among a selection of dishes to accompany rice. For the vegetarian Hindus, it is a popular everyday dish or a tasty snack, served with Indian flatbread. Made with firm vegetables, roots and gourds, all cut into long bitesize pieces, it is substantial and flexible – choose your own assortment of vegetables, such as pumpkin, butternut squash, winter melon, yams, aubergines (eggplants) or beans.

**1** Using a mortar and pestle or food processor, grind the chillies, ginger, roasted cumin seeds and sugar to a paste.

**2** In a heavy pan, bring 450ml/15fl oz/scant 2 cups water to the boil. Stir in the turmeric, cinnamon stick and salt. Add the carrots and cook for 1 minute. Add the sweet potatoes and cook for 2 minutes. Add the courgettes, plantain and beans and cook for a further 2 minutes. Reduce the heat, stir in the spice paste and curry leaves, and cook gently for 4–5 minutes, or until the vegetables are tender but not soft and mushy, and the liquid has greatly reduced.

**3** Gently stir in half the coconut. Take the pan off the heat and fold in the yogurt. Season to taste with salt and pepper. Quickly roast the remaining coconut in a heavy pan over a high heat, until nicely browned. Sprinkle a little over the *avial* in the pan, and serve the rest with spoonfuls of *avial* and flatbread.

**Cook's tip** Choose live yogurt if you can find it – the beneficial bacteria help to maintain good digestion.

### Serves four

2–3 green chillies, seeded and chopped

25g/1oz fresh root ginger, peeled and chopped

5–10ml/1–2 tsp roasted cumin seeds

10ml/2 tsp sugar

5–10ml/1–2 tsp ground turmeric

1 cinnamon stick

5ml/1 tsp salt

2 carrots, cut into bitesize sticks

2 sweet potatoes, cut into bitesize sticks

2 courgettes (zucchini), partially peeled in strips, seeded and cut into bitesize sticks

1 green plantain, peeled and cut into bitesize sticks

a small coil of snake beans (long beans) or a handful of green beans, cut into bitesize sticks

a handful fresh curry leaves

1 fresh coconut, grated

250ml/8fl oz/1 cup Greek (US strained plain) yogurt

salt and ground black pepper

Per Portion Energy 419Kcal/1753kJ; Protein 9.9g; Carbohydrate 47.7g, of which sugars 19.4g; Fat 23g, of which saturates 16.9g; Cholesterol 0mg; Calcium 176mg; Fibre 9g; Sodium 104mg.

**Serves four**

115g/4oz fresh coconut, grated

30ml/2 tbsp dried prawns (shrimp), soaked in warm water until soft

225g/8oz beansprouts, rinsed and drained

1 small cucumber, peeled, seeded and cut into julienne strips

2–3 spring onions (scallions), trimmed, cut into 2.5cm/1in pieces and halved lengthways

a handful of young, tender mangetouts (snow peas), halved diagonally

a handful of green beans, halved lengthways

a handful of fresh chives, chopped into 2.5cm/1in pieces

a handful of fresh mint leaves, finely chopped

2–3 red chillies, seeded and sliced finely lengthways

juice of 2 limes

10ml/2 tsp sugar

salt and ground black pepper

# Kerabu

Kelantan in the north of Malaysia is well known for its rich Malay cuisine, particularly *nasi kerabu*, the famous blue rice dish, and this beansprout salad, *kerabu*, which is served with it. In the Kota Bharu markets, up near the Thai border, the blue rice is wrapped in a banana leaf with *kerabu* and eaten as a snack – the first or last Malay snack when crossing the border. *Kerabu* is also served as a refreshing salad to accompany many of the highly spiced Malay dishes.

**1** Dry-roast the coconut in a heavy pan until it is lightly browned and emits a nutty aroma. Using a mortar and pestle or a food processor, grind the roasted coconut to a coarse powder. Drain the soaked dried prawns and grind them coarsely too.

**2** Put the vegetables, herbs and chillies into a bowl. Mix the lime juice with the sugar and pour it over the salad. Season with salt and pepper. Scatter the ground coconut and dried prawns over the salad, and toss well until thoroughly mixed.

**Per Portion** Energy 230Kcal/947kJ; Protein 12.6g; Carbohydrate 15.9g, of which sugars 13.9g; Fat 12.9g, of which saturates 10.2g; Cholesterol 0mg; Calcium 151mg; Fibre 7.8g; Sodium 24mg.

# Rojak

Originally from Indonesia, *rojak* has been so well integrated into the cuisine of Malaysia and Singapore that there is even an Indian version, also known as Singapore *rojak*, made with hard-boiled eggs, fried tofu, sliced fish cakes and a spicy sauce. The Chinese, Peranakans and Malays all have their own versions, varying from region to region, but all include a selection of fruit and vegetables, bathed in a tangy sauce. Perhaps the most famous is Penang *rojak*, which consists of crunchy *jicama*, green mango, pineapple and cucumber with a pungent chilli and peanut sauce. As this recipe is so flexible, you can really use any combination or fruit and vegetables and make the sauce as pungent and fiery as you like.

**1** First make the sauce. Using a mortar and pestle or food processor, grind the peanuts with the garlic and chillies to a coarse paste. Beat in the roasted shrimp paste, tamarind paste and sugar. Add enough water to make a thick, pouring sauce, and stir until the sugar has dissolved. Add salt to taste.

**2** Arrange the sliced fruit and vegetables on a plate, with the beansprouts scattered over the top. Drizzle the sauce over the salad and garnish with mint leaves. Serve with grilled meats and spicy dishes, or on its own as a healthy snack.

### Serves four to six

1 *jicama* (sweet turnip), peeled and finely sliced

1 small cucumber, partially peeled and finely sliced

1 green mango, peeled and finely sliced

1 star fruit (carambola), finely sliced

4 slices fresh pineapple, cored

half a pomelo, separated into segments, with membrane removed

a handful of beansprouts, rinsed and drained

fresh mint leaves, to garnish

### For the sauce

225g/8oz/2 cups roasted peanuts

4 garlic cloves, chopped

2–4 red chillies, seeded and chopped

10ml/2 tsp shrimp paste, dry-roasted in a pan over a high heat

15ml/1 tbsp tamarind paste

30ml/2 tbsp palm sugar

salt

**Per Portion** Energy 330Kcal/1381kJ; Protein 12.9g; Carbohydrate 28g, of which sugars 25.1g; Fat 19.3g, of which saturates 3.4g; Cholesterol 13mg; Calcium 114mg; Fibre 6.3g; Sodium 416mg.

# Fried tofu salad with a tangy sauce

A great favourite at the hawker stalls, fried tofu can either be stuffed with beansprouts and cucumber and then drizzled with a sauce, or it can be arranged as a salad on a plate. Either way *tahu goreng*, as this salad is known, is tangy and refreshing, an ideal accompaniment to grilled meats and stir-fried noodles. The Malays, Peranakans and Eurasians all enjoy this dish, so the sauce varies from stall to stall.

**Serves four**

vegetable oil, for deep-frying

450g/1lb firm rectangular tofu, rinsed, patted dry and cut into blocks

1 small cucumber, partially peeled in strips, seeded and shredded

2 spring onions (scallions), trimmed, halved and shredded

2 handfuls of fresh beansprouts rinsed and drained

fresh coriander (cilantro) leaves, to garnish

## For the sauce

30ml/2 tbsp tamarind pulp, soaked in water until soft

15ml/1 tbsp sesame or groundnut (peanut) oil

4 shallots, finely chopped

4 garlic cloves, finely chopped

2 red chillies, seeded

2.5ml/$\frac{1}{2}$ tsp shrimp paste

115g/4oz/1 cup roasted peanuts, crushed

30–45ml/2–3 tbsp *kecap manis*

15ml/1 tbsp tomato ketchup

**1** First make the sauce. Squeeze the tamarind pulp to soften it in the water, and then strain through a sieve (strainer). Measure out 120ml/4fl oz/$\frac{1}{2}$ cup tamarind pulp.

**2** Heat the oil in a wok or heavy pan, and stir in the shallots, garlic and chillies, until fragrant. Stir in the shrimp paste and the peanuts, until they emit a nutty aroma. Add the *kecap manis*, tomato ketchup and tamarind pulp and blend to form a thick sauce. Set aside and leave to cool.

**3** Heat enough oil for deep-frying in a wok or heavy pan. Slip in the blocks of tofu and fry until golden brown all over. Pat dry on kitchen paper and cut each block into slices. Arrange the slices on a plate with the cucumber, spring onions and beansprouts. Drizzle the sauce over the top or serve it separately in a bowl and garnish with the coriander leaves.

**Cook's tip** If you cannot find *kecap manis*, which consists of soy sauce sweetened with palm sugar, you could switch to ordinary soy sauce and increase the tomato ketchup to achieve a balance of sweet and sour in the sauce.

**Per Portion** Energy 423Kcal/1749kJ; Protein 17.9g; Carbohydrate 7.8g, of which sugars 4.5g; Fat 35.8g, of which saturates 5.3g; Cholesterol 0mg; Calcium 607mg; Fibre 2.8g; Sodium 296mg.

# Sweet snacks & drinks

# Sweet snacks & drinks

People of all cultures in Malaysia and Singapore love sweet foods and sugary drinks and there is no shortage of puddings, fresh, ripened exotic fruit, ice cream and other refreshing snacks made with ice. Some of the best sweet snacks can be sampled at the hawker stalls, and there are an amazing variety – each culinary tradition has its own distinctive specialities, some subtly aromatic, scented with rose petals, others richly sugary.

In general, the Chinese sweet stalls serve up a limited selection of soupy, or porridge-like, puddings made with glutinous rice or red, yellow or green beans, and a choice of steamed or boiled dumplings filled with sweet sesame or bean paste. The Malay and Peranakan stalls display a wider choice, ranging from sweet cakes, *kueh-kueh*, the deliciously moist sago pudding, *sagu gula melaka*, and the ubiquitous deep-fried bananas to *gulab jamun*, the Indian coconut balls fried in ghee and soaked in syrup, and *laddu*, another Indian pudding made with yellow lentils, cow's milk and sugar.

## Refreshing snacks

To cool you down in the heat of the day, the Malay stalls also produce a selection of sweet, refreshing snacks made with ice. *Ais kacang* consists of red beans, seaweed jelly and corn, in a pool of condensed milk, topped with shavings of ice and palm sugar syrup, whereas the popular *ais ball* is basically a ball of ice, filled with red beans and smeared in rose syrup, condensed milk and palm syrup. Ice cream is served between wafers or tucked into a slice of bread to make a sandwich.

In spite of people's sweet tooth, meals in Malaysia and Singapore rarely end with a dessert. Instead, they are polished off with ripe, juicy fruit, which ranges from crisp apples and honeydew melons, to dark purple mangosteens, red, hairy rambutans, bumpy pod-like jackfruit, and stinky durians. The sweet dishes, on the other hand, are enjoyed at any time of day for that little sugary burst of comfort and satisfaction.

Often found near the fruit stalls, the colourful fruits may be eaten just as they are, sliced and dipped in sauces or tossed in salads, and a few of the fleshy varieties are cooked with sugar to make a pudding. The white-fleshed rambutans are piled next to their relatives, the

juicy lychees; jackfruit are cut in half to reveal the sweet and fragrant yellow flesh, which is tossed in spicy salads or boiled with sugar to make puddings; wedges of scarlet watermelon are cut to quench the thirst; guavas are sliced and served with sweet-and-sour plum powder; unripe star fruit (carambola) is dipped in salt to enhance the flavour; the pink, bell-shaped *jambu* (rose apples) are dipped in soy sauce spiked with chillies; mangosteens are paired with the king of fruit, the durian. This has a pungent-sweet flesh, which can be eaten raw or cooked, in recipes such as the porridge-like *durian pengat*, made with coconut cream and palm sugar. At some of the Malay stalls,

**Right** *Ice creams are made from coconut and other exotic fruits.*

*Left Lychees (left) and passion fruit are used to make elegant little puddings.*

durian flesh is added to the iced dessert, *ais kacang*, and to Chinese moon cakes. Fermented durian pulp, *tempoyak*, is an acquired taste but much appreciated in rural Malaysia, particularly in Sabah and Sarawak, where it is added to curries and *sambals*. The Malays are in no doubt that durian serves as a powerful aphrodisiac: the local saying is, "'When the durians go down, the sarongs go up!".

## Juice drinks

Drink carts are another feature of the street markets, food halls and shopping centres in Malaysia and Singapore. With such a wealth of home-grown fruits, there are plenty to squeeze or blend into refreshing drinks to cool down passers-by in the heat and humidity. Fruits such as pineapples, mangoes and watermelons are blended to make delicious concoctions – the local favourite in Singapore is made with carrots and oranges; sugar cane is pressed to extract sweet juice, which is served with a wedge of lemon; lime juice, pressed from the tiny, dark green *kalamansi* limes with their pale orange flesh, is served in coffee shops as a palate soother and cleanser when eating curry and spicy dishes. Coconut

water, served in the actual coconut, is also regarded as a tamer of the palate. When served at roadside stalls in Malaysia, the tops of green coconuts are carved to a point and the tip is lobbed off to enable you to drink the water and eat the flesh at the same time.

The drink stalls and carts also produce a variety of sweet drinks that are more like snacks in their consistency. The Malay favourite, *air bandung*, is a sweet condensed milk drink, flavoured with pink rose syrup and served chilled; *air soya* is a protein-enriched, soya bean milk drink, which can be drunk hot or cold; *air cincau* is considered a herbal tonic as it is made with a pandanus-flavoured syrup containing strands of black jelly, *agar-agar*, which is obtained from seaweed; and avocados are blended with condensed milk to make thick, nourishing milkshakes.

Leaning towards the category of a sweet snack, rather than a drink, is *candol*. This is made by placing fine mung bean noodles into the bottom quarter of a glass, followed by palm sugar syrup, coconut milk, and topped with shavings of ice. The idea is to eat the noodles with a spoon and then drink the liquid. Also available at stalls and coffee shops are *air mata kuching*, a kind of Chinese tea made from boiling red dates and dried longans in water, and *lassi*, an Indian yogurt-based drink which is commonly served with Indian food. The Malays and Indonesians also

enjoy their own version of *lassi*, which can be sweet or savoury, flavoured with mint, puréed mango or rose water.

## Alcoholic beverages

In general, alcohol is frowned upon in Malaysia, given the predominantly Muslim foundation of the culture. Exceptions to the rule are the non-Muslim peoples of Sarawak and Sabah, who indulge in their local beverages of palm-sap and rice wine. In Singapore, where there is a high Chinese population and a significant number of Catholic Eurasians and international residents, alcohol is consumed more liberally. Chinese wine, local beers, wines and cocktails, such as Singapore Sling, are all available in the restaurants and hotels.

As the Malays and Chinese believe in the restorative and rejuvenating qualities of particular plants, a root found in the rainforests is used to make an aphrodisiac drink that is popular in the coffee shops and hawker stalls!

*Right Lassi flavoured with rosewater makes a fragrant, cooling drink.*

# Roasted coconut ice cream

The popularity of ice cream in Malaysia and Singapore ensures that, in the cities at least, you will not have to search for it. Ice cream trucks set themselves up at busy street corners, shopping centres and entertainment parks selling an exotic selection, with flavours ranging from passion fruit, mango, sour plum and durian to coconut, avocado and corn.

**Serves four to six**

115g/4oz fresh coconut, finely chopped in a food processor

4 large (US extra large) egg yolks

115g/4oz/generous $^1/_2$ cup sugar

900ml/1$^1/_2$ pints/3$^3/_4$ cups coconut milk

250ml/8fl oz/1 cup double (heavy) cream

25ml/1$^1/_2$ tbsp rice flour, blended with 30ml/2 tbsp coconut milk or cream

salt

**1** Roast the coconut in a heavy frying pan over a medium heat until nicely browned and emitting a nutty aroma. Transfer to a plate and leave to cool.

**2** In a bowl, whisk the egg yolks with the sugar until pale and creamy. In a heavy pan, heat the coconut milk with the cream and a generous pinch of salt to scalding point. Gradually pour the hot coconut milk into the egg yolk mixture, whisking vigorously at the same time to form a smooth custard. Strain the custard into a clean heavy pan and stir it gently over a low heat, until slightly thickened.

**3** Beat the rice flour mixture into the custard until it coats the back of a wooden spoon. Pour the custard into a bowl or freezer-proof container and leave to cool.

**4** Stir most of the roasted coconut (reserve a little for decorating) into the cooled custard and put it in the freezer until frozen, taking it out and stirring after about half an hour. Alternatively, churn in an ice cream maker according to the manufacturer's instructions.

**5** To serve, sprinkle the ice cream with the reserved roasted coconut.

**Per Portion** Energy 448Kcal/1863kJ; Protein 4.1g; Carbohydrate 32.5g, of which sugars 29.1g; Fat 34.3g, of which saturates 21.9g; Cholesterol 192mg; Calcium 95mg; Fibre 1.8g; Sodium 191mg.

# Sweet puréed avocado

This sweet avocado snack is thought to have originated with the Dutch in Melaka, but now it is also served in Penang and Singapore, where it is popular with the sweet-toothed Malays, Indians, Eurasians and, of course, tourists. It can be served as a thick purée or blended with coconut milk until it is the consistency of thick pouring cream. It can be enjoyed as a drink with a couple of ice cubes stirred in.

**1** Put the avocado flesh into a food processor and purée it with the lime juice. Add the condensed milk, coconut cream and salt and process until the mixture is smooth and creamy.

**2** Spoon the mixture into individual bowls or glasses and chill over ice. Decorate with a few mint leaves and serve with lime wedges to squeeze over it.

**Serves two**

1 avocado, stoned (pitted)

juice of $1/2$ lime

30ml/2 tbsp sweetened condensed milk

30ml/2 tbsp coconut cream

a pinch of salt

fresh mint leaves, to decorate

$1/2$ lime, halved, to serve

**Variation** This recipe works equally well with other soft-fleshed fruit, such as bananas, mango and papaya.

**Per Portion** Energy 243Kcal/1006kJ; Protein 3.2g; Carbohydrate 10.3g, of which sugars 9.2g; Fat 21.2g, of which saturates 8.5g; Cholesterol 5mg; Calcium 54mg; Fibre 2.6g; Sodium 421mg.

# Pumpkin, sweet potato and banana in coconut milk

This dish of sweet vegetables cooked with bananas in coconut milk is a favourite among many rural Malays and Indonesians. Served as a sweet snack, or for breakfast, it is both nourishing and warming. It is also a popular sweet food in the jungles and fields of Sarawak, Sabah and the rural areas of the Malaysian peninsula, with the recipes differing by the inclusion of gourds such as yam, butternut squash and winter melon.

**1** Pour the coconut milk into a heavy pan and bring it to the boil. Stir in the pumpkin, sweet potatoes and pandanus leaf. Continue to boil for 1 minute, then reduce the heat and simmer for about 15 minutes, until the pumpkin and sweet potato are tender but not too soft.

**2** Using a slotted spoon, lift the pumpkin and sweet potato pieces out of the coconut milk and put them on a plate. Add the sugar and salt to the coconut milk and stir until the sugar has dissolved. Bring the sweetened coconut milk to the boil, then reduce the heat and simmer for 5 minutes.

**3** Add the bananas to the sweetened coconut milk and simmer for 4 minutes. Put the pumpkin and sweet potato back into the pan and gently mix all the ingredients together. Remove the pandanus leaf and serve warm.

**Serves four to six**

900ml/1½ pints/3¾ cups coconut milk

½ small pumpkin, seeded and cut into bitesize cubes

2 sweet potatoes, cut into bitesize pieces

1 pandanus (screwpine) leaf

150g/5oz/¾ cup palm sugar

2.5ml/½ tsp salt

3 bananas, cut into thick diagonal slices

**Per Portion** Energy 249Kcal/1063kJ; Protein 2.6g; Carbohydrate 61.4g, of which sugars 51.7g; Fat 1g, of which saturates 0.5g; Cholesterol 0mg; Calcium 97mg; Fibre 2.8g; Sodium 187mg.

**Serves four**

115g/4oz fresh root ginger, chopped

400ml/14fl oz/1²/₃ cups coconut milk

60ml/4 tbsp sugar

2 egg whites

# Steamed ginger custards

Delicate and warming, ginger custard is a favourite among the Chinese and Peranakans in Singapore. Often served warm, straight from the steamer, the individual custards are enjoyed as a sweet mid-afternoon snack or even late at night. They are equally delightful served cold as a dessert.

**1** Using a mortar and pestle or food processor, grind the ginger to a fine paste. Press the ginger paste through a fine sieve (strainer), or twist it in a piece of muslin (cheesecloth), to extract the juice.

**2** Fill a wok one-third of the way up with water. Place a bamboo steamer in the wok, bring the water to the boil and reduce the heat to low.

**3** In a bowl, whisk the coconut milk, sugar and egg whites with the ginger juice until the mixture is smooth and the sugar has dissolved. Pour the mixture into four individual heatproof bowls and place them in the steamer. Cover and steam for 15–20 minutes, until the mixture sets.

**4** Remove the bowls from the steamer and leave to cool. Cover them with clear film (plastic wrap) and place in the refrigerator overnight. Serve the custards chilled or at room temperature.

**Per Portion** Energy 89Kcal/380kJ; Protein 2g; Carbohydrate 20.8g, of which sugars 20.8g; Fat 0.4g, of which saturates 0.2g; Cholesterol 0mg; Calcium 50mg; Fibre 0.3g; Sodium 159mg.

# Sticky coconut rice in banana leaves

Sweet and savoury sticky rice cooked in banana leaves is common fare in the markets and at the hawker stalls throughout South-east Asia. In this recipe, sliced banana is added to steamed rice to make this sweet treat particularly moist and delicious.

**Serves four**

115g/4oz/generous ½ cup white sticky rice, well rinsed in several changes of water, soaked in plenty of water for 6 hours and drained

400ml/14fl oz/1⅔ cups coconut milk

60ml/4 tbsp palm sugar

banana leaves, cut into pieces, roughly 20cm/8 in square

2 bananas, cut into diagonal slices

salt

coconut cream and icing (confectioners') sugar, to serve

**Banana leaf bundles** In the north of the Malaysian peninsula, where much of the rice is grown and the influence from Thailand is strong, these little banana leaf bundles are very popular snacks. They are also in demand at the Malay hawker stalls in fast-paced Kuala Lumpur and Singapore.

**1** Fill a wok one-third of the way up with water and place a bamboo steamer inside it. Bring the water to the boil and place a piece of muslin (cheesecloth), dampened in warm water, over the rack. Spread the sticky rice on it, leaving a gap at the edges for the steam to come through. Fold over the edges of the muslin, place the lid on the steamer, and leave to steam for about 20 minutes until the rice is tender but still firm.

**2** Meanwhile, heat the coconut milk in a heavy pan with the sugar and a pinch of salt, stirring all the time until the sugar has dissolved. Stir in the steamed sticky rice until well mixed. Remove from the heat, cover the pan and leave the rice to sit for 10–15 minutes until it has absorbed the sweetened coconut milk.

**3** Place the banana leaf squares on a flat surface. Spread 30ml/2 tbsp of rice in the centre of each, in the shape of a rectangle. Place a few overlapping banana slices on top and form a sandwich with another 30ml/2 tbsp rice. Fold in the two short ends, and then fold over the wider flaps to form a bundle. Secure the bundle with string or a cocktail stick (toothpick).

**4** Make sure the wok is filled one-third of the way up with water. Place the bundles in the bamboo steamer, cover with the lid and steam for 1 hour. Serve the bundles hot, straight from the steamer, with a dollop of coconut cream and a dusting of icing sugar, or leave them to cool in the banana leaves and serve at room temperature as a sweet snack.

**Per Portion** Energy 232Kcal/981kJ; Protein 3.1g; Carbohydrate 55.1g, of which sugars 31g; Fat 0.6g, of which saturates 0.3g; Cholesterol 0mg; Calcium 46mg; Fibre 0.6g; Sodium 112mg.

# Jellied mango puddings with tropical fruits

Light and sophisticated, these jellied mango puddings make delightful desserts. Served with a selection of tropical fruits, they add a refreshing touch to the end of a spicy meal. You are more likely to find these elegant little puddings in the dim sum restaurants in Singapore and Kuala Lumpur, than as a sweet snack at a hawker stall.

**1** In a heavy pan, heat the coconut milk with the sugar, stirring all the time, until it has dissolved. Add the gelatine and keep stirring until it has dissolved. Remove from the heat. Beat the egg yolk with the mango purée. Add the purée to the coconut milk and stir until smooth. Spoon the mixture into individual, lightly oiled moulds and leave to cool. Place them in the refrigerator for 2–3 hours, until set.

### Serves four

750ml/1¼ pints/3 cups coconut milk

150g/5oz/¾ cup sugar

15ml/1 tbsp powdered gelatine (gelatin)

1 egg yolk

1 large, ripe mango, stoned (pitted) and puréed

4 slices ripe jackfruit or pineapple, quartered

1 banana, cut into diagonal slices

1 kiwi fruit, sliced

4 lychees, peeled

2 passion fruit, split open, to decorate

**2** To serve, arrange the fruit on individual plates, leaving enough room for the jellies. Dip the base of each mould briefly into hot water, and then invert the puddings on to the plates. Lift off the moulds and decorate with passion fruit seeds.

**Variation** The tangy fruitiness of mango is particularly delicious in these jellied puddings, but you could substitute papaya, banana, durian or avocado.

**Per Portion** Energy 305Kcal/1300kJ; Protein 2.9g; Carbohydrate 72.6g, of which sugars 72g; Fat 2.4g, of which saturates 0.8g; Cholesterol 50mg; Calcium 109mg; Fibre 3g; Sodium 216mg.

# Sago pudding with palm sugar syrup

In Sabah and Sarawak, sago is the main staple, used in savoury and sweet dishes, such as this one. However, this sweet pudding, *sagu gula melaka*, is enjoyed in many Malay homes throughout the Peninsula.

**1** Bring a deep pan of water to the boil. Drop in the pandanus leaf and let the sago pour into the water through the fingertips of one hand, while you stir with a wooden spoon with the other hand, to prevent the pearls from sticking. Boil for 5 minutes, then remove from the heat, cover the pan and leave the sago to steam for about 10 minutes – the pearls should be swollen and translucent. Drain the sago through a sieve (strainer) and rinse under running cold water.

**2** Reserve the pandanus leaf and put the sago into a bowl. Stir in 15–30ml/1–2 tbsp of the coconut milk – enough to bind it together –with a pinch of salt. Spoon the sago into a lightly greased mould, or four separate moulds, packing it down gently, and leave it to set at room temperature.

**3** Meanwhile, make the syrup. Put the water and palm sugar into a heavy pan and stir over a high heat until the sugar has dissolved. Bring to the boil and boil for 2 minutes. Drop in the reserved pandanus leaf, reduce the heat, and simmer for 10 minutes, stirring from time to time.

**4** Beat the rest of the coconut milk with a pinch of salt. Turn the mould, or individual moulds, upside down in a shallow bowl and slip them off the pudding. Spoon the coconut milk over the top, allowing it to flow down the sides and form a pool in the dish, and pour over the hot syrup. Serve immediately, while the syrup is still hot.

**Variations** Alternatively, you could keep the sago hot in a steamer and heat up the coconut milk, so that the whole pudding is hot. If you cannot find pandanus leaves, use a vanilla pod (bean) for flavouring instead.

### Serves four

1 pandanus (screwpine) leaf, tied in a knot

250g/9oz pearl sago, picked over, washed and drained

400ml/14fl oz/1²/₃ cups coconut milk, lightly beaten

salt

### For the syrup

250ml/8fl oz/1 cup water

175g/6oz/³/₄ cup palm sugar

**Per Portion** Energy 416Kcal/1777kJ; Protein 0.7g; Carbohydrate 109.4g, of which sugars 50.6g; Fat 0.4g, of which saturates 0.2g; Cholesterol 0mg; Calcium 59mg; Fibre 0.3g; Sodium 115mg.

## Red bean pudding

Chinese in origin but popular throughout South-east Asia, the tiny red azuki beans are often served as a sweet snack. Red, yellow and green beans are used in many Chinese sweet dishes, such as the syrupy soups or spongy dumplings filled with bean paste. At some of the hawker stalls, this pudding is presented on a banana leaf with a drizzle of coconut milk.

**Serves four to six**

115g/4oz dried red azuki beans, soaked in water for 2 hours

1.2 litres/2 pints/5 cups water

4 pandanus (screwpine) leaves

150g/5oz/$^3$/$_4$ cup sugar

150ml/5fl oz/$^2$/$_3$ cup thick coconut milk, fresh or canned, beaten until smooth, or fresh coconut cream

**1** Drain the soaked beans and put them in a deep pan. Add the water and bring it to the boil. Add the pandanus leaves and reduce the heat. Simmer uncovered for about 40 minutes until the beans are tender and the water has greatly reduced.

**2** Stir in the sugar until it has dissolved, and simmer for a further 10 minutes. Remove the pandanus leaves and spoon the sweetened beans into individual bowls. Serve hot or leave to cool and chill in the refrigerator before serving. Serve the coconut milk or cream separately, to pour over.

**Variation** Generally, pandanus leaves are used to flavour the syrup in this dish but you could easily use a flavouring of your choice, such as fresh root ginger, bay or lime leaves, lemon grass or vanilla.

**Per Portion** Energy 155Kcal/661kJ; Protein 4.4g; Carbohydrate 35.8g, of which sugars 27.8g; Fat 0.4g, of which saturates 0.1g; Cholesterol 0mg; Calcium 40mg; Fibre 3g; Sodium 33mg.

# Deep-fried bananas with coconut

Perhaps the most common of all the sweet snacks, deep-fried bananas are popular throughout South-east Asia, and are a hawker-stall favourite in Malaysia and Singapore. Versatile and delicious, they are often munched on their own, sprinkled with sugar, or they can be served with sweet sticky rice, ice creams or steamed cakes and buns.

**1** Sift the flour with the baking powder and a pinch of salt into a bowl. Make a well in the centre and drop in the eggs. Gradually pour in the coconut milk, beating all the time, until the batter is thick and smooth.

**2** Beat in the sugar and fresh dessicated coconut and add the banana pieces, coating them gently with the batter.

**3** Heat enough oil for deep-frying in a wok or large heavy pan. Check the oil is the right temperature by dropping in a cube of bread – if it sizzles and turns golden brown, the oil is ready. Lift the pieces of banana out of the batter with tongs or chopsticks and lower them into the oil. Fry two or three pieces at a time, until crisp and golden, and drain on kitchen paper. Repeat with the remaining banana pieces. Sprinkle sugar over the bananas and serve while still warm.

**Serves four to six**

115g/4oz/1 cup plain (all-purpose) or rice flour

5ml/1 tsp baking powder

2 eggs

750ml/1¼ pints/3 cups coconut milk

30ml/2 tbsp palm or granulated sugar

90g/3½oz fresh coconut, grated or desiccated (dry unsweetened shredded) coconut

3 large bananas, halved widthways and lengthways

vegetable oil, for deep-frying

salt

caster (superfine) or icing (confectioners') sugar, for sprinkling

**Per Portion** Energy 377Kcal/1571kJ; Protein 5g; Carbohydrate 39.6g, of which sugars 22.7g; Fat 22.5g, of which saturates 9.9g; Cholesterol 63mg; Calcium 26mg; Fibre 3.2g; Sodium 30mg.

**Serves two**

300ml/½ pint/1¼ cups natural (plain) yogurt

5–10ml/1–2 tsp rose essence

10ml/2 tsp sugar

6 ice cubes, to serve

rose petals, to decorate

# Rose-flavoured *lassi*

Sweet and savoury *lassi* is always in demand at Indian and Malay coffee shops, restaurants and hawker stalls. Soothing and cooling, this Indian yogurt-based drink is an ideal partner to spicy food. Savoury *lassi* is often salty and flavoured with mint, whereas the sweet drink is fragrant with the traditional essences of rose or pandanus.

**1** In a jug (pitcher), beat the yogurt with 150ml/¼ pint/⅔ cup water, until smooth. Add the rose essence and sugar, adjusting the sweetness to taste, and mix well.

**2** Divide the ice cubes between two glasses and pour in the *lassi*. Decorate with a few rose petals and serve.

**Per Portion** Energy 104Kcal/438kJ; Protein 7.7g; Carbohydrate 16.5g, of which sugars 16.5g; Fat 1.5g, of which saturates 0.8g; Cholesterol 2mg; Calcium 288mg; Fibre 0g; Sodium 125mg.

# Singapore Sling

Needless to say, this drink is from Singapore. However, it is not really drunk by the Singapore locals, who are largely Chinese, Peranakans, Muslim Malays and Hindu Indians. Some local businessmen may partake in a beer or a glass of wine now and then, but cocktails like this are really for the tourists. It is on offer in every high-class hotel and restaurant, some even specialize in it.

**1** Place the ice cubes in a tall cocktail glass. Pour in the gin, grenadine and sweet and sour. Fill the glass up with soda water. Splash in the cherry brandy and top with the cherry. Serve immediately with a straw.

**Sweet and sour** This is also known as sour mix, sweet and sour mix or bar mix. It is a mixer made of lemon or lime juice and sugar syrup and is an important part of many cocktails. To make your own, mix one part heavy sugar syrup (3 parts sugar, 2 parts water) with one part lemon juice, and add 2 egg whites per 1 litre/1¾ pints/4 cups of mix. The egg whites are optional; they will make the drinks slightly foamy. You may want to adjust the sugar/juice ratio for the right balance of sweetness and tartness.

**Serves one**

ice cubes

30ml/2 tbsp gin

15ml/1 tbsp grenadine

50ml/2fl oz/¼ cup sweet and sour

30ml/2 tbsp cherry brandy

soda water

1 maraschino cherry, to decorate

**Per Portion** Energy 309Kcal/1296kJ; Protein 0g; Carbohydrate 35.5g, of which sugars 35.4g; Fat 0g, of which saturates 0g; Cholesterol 0mg; Calcium 3mg; Fibre 0g; Sodium 48mg.

# Essential condiments

# Sambal belacan

This is the ubiquitous condiment of the Malays and Peranakans. As they have such a penchant for strong, fiery tastes, this pungent condiment graces their tables on a daily basis. A little dollop seems to go with everything: chunks of bread, rice, grilled foods, and stir-fried vegetables.

**1** In a small, heavy pan, dry-roast the shrimp paste until it is aromatic and crumbly. Using a mortar and pestle or food processor, grind the roasted shrimp paste with the chillies to form a paste. Grind in half the chilli seeds and the lime leaves.

**2** Add the sugar and salt, and stir in the rest of the chilli seeds. Moisten with the lime juice. Spoon the *sambal* into little dishes and serve with wedges of lime to squeeze over it.

**Serves four**

15ml/1 tbsp shrimp paste

4 fresh red chillies, seeded (reserve the seeds)

2 kaffir lime leaves, spines removed, and chopped

2.5ml/$\frac{1}{2}$ tsp sugar

1.5ml/$\frac{1}{4}$ tsp salt

juice of 1 lime

1 lime, quartered, to serve

**Cook's tip** The fermented shrimp paste, *belacan*, is available in South-east Asian markets. If you cannot get hold of it, replace it with the readily available Thai shrimp paste.

**Per Portion** Energy 17Kcal/69kJ; Protein 2.8g; Carbohydrate 0.8g, of which sugars 0.8g; Fat 0.3g, of which saturates 0g; Cholesterol 19mg; Calcium 53mg; Fibre 0g; Sodium 312mg.

**Serves four**

5ml/1 tsp shrimp paste

4 fresh red chillies, seeded

7.5ml/1¹⁄₂ tsp salt

5ml/1 tsp sugar

1 green mango, peeled and shredded

juice of ¹⁄₂ lime

# Sour mango *sambal*

Another Malay favourite is *sambal asam*, sour *sambal*, made with green mango or papaya. It is served in small quantities as a relish to accompany fried fish and shellfish, spicy grilled foods, and fiery curries, but it can also be served on its own as a refreshing snack.

**1** In a small, heavy pan, dry-roast the shrimp paste until it is aromatic and crumbly.

**2** Using a mortar and pestle or food processor, grind the chillies with the salt to form a paste. Add the shrimp paste and sugar and pound into the spicy paste. Toss in the shredded mango and moisten with the lime juice. Mix well and serve in little bowls.

**Per Portion** Energy 34Kcal/143kJ; Protein 1.7g; Carbohydrate 6.5g, of which sugars 6.4g; Fat 0.3g, of which saturates 0.1g; Cholesterol 6mg; Calcium 28mg; Fibre 1g; Sodium 794mg.

# Pineapple pickle

This spicy sweet-and-sour pickle is ideal to serve with spicy grilled foods or as an accompaniment to curries or vegetable dishes.

**1** In a small, heavy pan, dry-roast the mustard seeds until they pop.

**2** Using a mortar and pestle or food processor, grind the chillies, ginger and garlic to a paste. Stir in the mustard seeds and ground turmeric. Add the vinegar and sugar, stirring until the sugar has completely dissolved.

**3** Put the pineapple in a bowl and pour over the pickling sauce. Add salt to taste. The pickle will keep for 2–3 days in the refrigerator.

**Serves six to eight**

15ml/1 tbsp brown mustard seeds

2 dried chillies, soaked in water until soft, seeded, and squeezed dry

15g/½oz fresh root ginger, peeled and chopped

1 garlic clove, chopped

5ml/1 tsp ground turmeric

200ml/7fl oz/scant 1 cup white wine vinegar or rice vinegar

15ml/1 tbsp palm sugar

1 ripe pineapple, peeled, cored and diced

salt

**Condiments** The Malays and Indians often serve a selection of condiments with every meal. There is the Malay *sambal*, the Nonya *acar* and myriad Indian pickles or chutneys, all of which can be interchanged with the spicy food of these cultures.

**Per Portion** Energy 56Kcal/238kJ; Protein 0.7g; Carbohydrate 12.5g, of which sugars 12.2g; Fat 0.2g, of which saturates 0g; Cholesterol 0mg; Calcium 20mg; Fibre 1.3g; Sodium 4mg.

## Serves eight to ten

8–10 limes

30ml/2 tbsp salt

150ml/5fl oz/²⁄₃ cup sesame or groundnut (peanut) oil

10–15ml/2–3 tsp brown mustard seeds

3–4 garlic cloves, cut into thin sticks

25g/1oz fresh root ginger, peeled and cut into thin sticks

5ml/1 tsp coriander seeds

5ml/1 tsp cumin seeds

5ml/1 tsp fennel seeds

10ml/2 tsp ground turmeric

10ml/2 tsp hot chilli powder or paste

a handful of fresh or dried curry leaves

**To serve**  This pickle is delicious served with grilled or fried fish, and spicy stir-fried noodles. You can make it as fiery as you like by adding more chilli powder.

# Lime pickle

This Indian pickle is popular among the Malays, Eurasians and Peranakans, as well as the Indian communities. Often sold in jars at hawker stalls, the pickle is reserved mainly as an accompaniment to fiery curries.

**1** Put the whole limes in a bowl. Cover with boiling water and leave to stand for 30 minutes. Drain the limes and cut each into quarters. Rub the lime pieces with salt and put them into a sealed sterilized jar. Leave the limes to cure in the salt for 1 week.

**2** Heat the oil in a wok and stir in the mustard seeds. When they begin to pop, stir in the garlic, ginger, spices and curry leaves. Cook gently for a few minutes to flavour the oil, then stir in the lime pieces and the juices from the jar. Reduce the heat and simmer for about 45 minutes, stirring from time to time. Store the pickle in sterilized jars and keep in a cool place for 1–2 months.

**Per Portion** Energy 96Kcal/395kJ; Protein 0.3g; Carbohydrate 0.9g, of which sugars 0.6g; Fat 10.1g, of which saturates 1.5g; Cholesterol 0mg; Calcium 25mg; Fibre 0.2g; Sodium 1185mg.

# Nonya *acar*

There are numerous versions of *acar*, a table pickle created in the Nonya kitchens. *Penang acar, acar Kunin* and *acar awak* all consist of a medley of vegetables which can be served as a relish or a side dish. More elaborate than the Malay and Indian pickles, Nonya *acar* recipes vary from household to household, so you can experiment with your own choice of vegetables.

**1** Put the vegetables into a bowl, sprinkle with salt and set aside for about 15 minutes. Rinse the vegetables, drain and pat dry.

**2** Using a mortar and pestle or a food processor, grind the chillies, garlic, ginger and turmeric to a smooth paste.

**3** Heat the oil in a wok. Stir in the shallots and lemon grass and fry until golden. Stir in the spice paste and fry until fragrant. Add the vegetables, tossing them around the wok to coat them in the spices. Add the vinegar and sugar and continue to cook the vegetables until they are tender, with just a bite to them.

**4** Season to taste with salt and put the vegetables into a large serving bowl. Leave to cool, then toss in the peanuts and sesame seeds.

**To store** Keep the pickle in a non-metallic container in the refrigerator, or a cool place, for 3–4 days.

## Serves six to ten

450g/1lb carrots, peeled and cut into matchsticks

450g/1lb daikon (white radish), peeled and cut into matchsticks

2 small cucumbers, halved lengthways, seeded and cut into matchsticks

6 dried red chillies, soaked in warm water to soften, seeded and squeezed dry

6 garlic cloves, chopped

50g/2oz fresh root ginger, peeled and chopped

50g/2oz fresh turmeric, chopped

30ml/2 tbsp vegetable or groundnut (peanut) oil

6 shallots, sliced

2 lemon grass stalks, halved and bruised

45–60ml/3–4 tbsp rice or white wine vinegar

30ml/2 tbsp sugar

45ml/3 tbsp roasted peanuts

30ml/2 tbsp roasted sesame seeds

salt

**Per Portion** Energy 96Kcal/398kJ; Protein 2.3g; Carbohydrate 9.6g, of which sugars 8.8g; Fat 5.6g, of which saturates 0.9g; Cholesterol 0mg; Calcium 52mg; Fibre 2.3g; Sodium 18mg.

# Suppliers

### Australia

Asian Supermarkets Pty Ltd
116 Charters Towers Road
Townsville QLD 4810
Tel: (07) 4772 3997

Burlington Supermarkets
Chinatown Mall
Fortitude Valley QLD 4006
Tel: (07) 3216 1828

Duc Hung Long Asian Store
95 The Crescent
Fairfield NSW 2165
Tel: (02) 9728 1092

Exotic Asian Groceries Q
    Supercentre
Cnr Market and Bermuda Sts
Mermaid Waters QLD 4218
Tel: (07) 5572 8188

Harris Farm Markets
Sydney Markets
Flemongton NSW 2140
Tel: (02) 9746 2055

Kongs Trading Pty Ltd
8 Kingscote Street
Kewdale WA 6105
Tel: (08) 9353 3380

Saigon Asian Food
6 Cape Street
Dickson ACT 2602
Tel: (02) 6247 4251

The Spice and Herb Asian
    Shop
200 Old Cleveland Road
Capalaba QLD 4157
Tel: (07) 3245 5300

Sydney Fish Market Pty Ltd
Cnr Pyrmont Bridge Road
    and Bank Street
Pyrmont NSW 2009
Tel: (02) 9660 1611

### United Kingdom

Good Harvest Fish Market
14 Newport Place
London WC2H 7PR
Tel: 020 7437 0712

Golden Gate Supermarket
16 Newport Place
London WC2H 7JS
Tel: 020 7437 6266

Hopewell Emporium
2f Dyne Road
London NW6 7XB
Tel: 020 7624 5473

Loon–Fung Supermarket
42-44 Gerrard Street
London W1V 7LP
Tel: 020 7437 7332

Manila Supermarket
11–12 Hogarth Place
London SW5 0QT
Tel: 020 7373 8305

Miah, A. and Co
20 Magdalen Street
Norwich NR3 1HE
Tel: 01603 615395

New Peking Supermarket
59 Westbourne Grove
London W2 4UA
Tel: 020 7928 8770

Newport Supermarket
28–29 Newport Court
London WC2H 7PQ
Tel: 020 7437 2386

Rum Wong Supermarket
London Road
Guildford GU1 2AF
Tel: 01483 451568

Seasoned Pioneers Ltd
101 Summers Road
Brunswick Business Park
Liverpool L3 4BJ
Tel: 0151 709 9330

S. W. Trading Ltd
Horn Lane
London SE10 0RT
Tel: 020 8293 9393

Tawana
18–20 Chepstow Road
London W2 5BD
Tel: 020 7221 6316

Wang Thai Supermarket
101 Kew Road
Twickenham
Surrey TW9 2PN
Tel: 020 8332 2959

Wing Tai
11a Aylesham Centre
Rye Lane
London SE15 5EW
Tel: 020 7635 0714

Wing Yip
395 Edgware Road
London NW2 6LN
Tel: 020 7450 0422
*also at*
Oldham Road
Ancoats
Manchester M4 5HU
Tel: 0161 832 3215
*and*
375 Nechells Park Road
Nechells
Birmingham B7 5NT
Tel: 0121 327 3838

*Mail Order Companies*

Fiddes Payne Herbs
   and Spices Ltd
Unit 3B, Thorpe Way
Banbury
Oxfordshire OX16 8XL
Tel: 01295 253 888

Fox's Spices
Mason's Road
Stratford-upon-Avon
Warwickshire CV37 9XN
Tel: 01789 266 420

## United States

Ai Hoa
860 North Hill Street
Los Angeles, CA 90026
Tel: (213) 482-4824

Asian Food Market
6450 Market Street
Upper Darby, PA 19082
Tel: (610) 352-4433

Asian Foods, Etc.
1375 Prince Avenue
Atlanta, GA 30341
Tel: (404) 543-8624

Asian Foods Ltd.
260-280 West Lehigh Avenue
Philadelphia, PA 19133
Tel: (215) 291-9500

Asian Market
2513 Stewart Avenue
Las Vegas, NV 89101
Tel: (702) 387-3373

Asian Market
18815 Eureka Road
South Gate, MI 48195
Fax: (734) 246-4795
www.asianmarket.qpg.com

Augusta Market Oriental
   Foods
2117 Martin Luther King Jr.
   Boulevard
Atlanta, GA 30901
Tel: (706) 722-4988

Bachri's Chili & Spice
   Gourmet
5617 Villa Haven
Pittsburgh, PA 15236
Tel: (412) 831-1131
Fax: (412) 831-2542

Bangkok Market
4757 Melrose Avenue
Los Angeles, CA 90029
Tel: (203) 662-7990

Bharati Food & Spice Center
6163 Reynolds Road Suite G
Morrow, GA 30340
Tel: (770) 961-9007

First Asian Food Center
3420 East Ponce De Leon Ave
Scottsdale, GA 30079
Tel: (404) 292-6508

Han Me Oriental Food & Gifts
2 E. Derenne Avenue
Savannah, GA 31405
Tel: (912) 355-6411

Hong Tan Oriental Food
2802 Capitol Street
Savannah, GA 31404
Tel: (404) 233-9184

The House of Rice Store
3221 North Hayden Road
Scottsdale, AZ 85251
Tel: (480) 947-6698

Huy Fong Foods Inc.
5001 Earle Avenue
Rosemead, CA 91770
Tel: (626) 286-8328

Khanh Tam Oriental Market
4051 Buford Highway NE
Atlanta, GA 30345
Tel: (404) 728-0393

May's American Oriental
Market
422 West University Avenue
Saint Paul, MN 55103
Tel: (651) 293-1118

Norcross Oriental Market
6062 Norcross-Tucker Road
Chamblee, GA 30341
Tel: (770) 496-1656

Oriental Grocery
11827 Del Amo Boulevard
Cerritos, CA 90701
Tel: (310) 924-1029

Oriental Market
670 Central Park Avenue
Yonkers, NY 10013
Tel: (212) 349-1979

The Oriental Pantry
423 Great Road
Acton, MA 01720
Tel: (978) 264-4576

Saigon Asian Market
10090 Central Avenue
Biloxi, MS 39532
Tel: (228) 392-8044

Siam Market
27266 East Baseline Street
Highland, CA 92346
Tel: (909) 862-8060

Unimart American
   and Asian Groceries
1201 Howard Street
San Francisco, CA 94103
Tel: (415) 431-0362

158

# Index